CW00409399

A Doctor to Defend
The Binayak Sen Story

A DOCTOR to DEFEND

The Binayak Sen Story

Minnie Vaid

Price: ₹350/- (Three Hundred Fifty Rupees)
Edition: 2011 © Minnie Vaid
ISBN: 978-81-7028-927-2
A DOCTOR TO DEFEND: The Binayak Sen Story
by Minnie Vaid
Cover design: Sakshi Chopra Kumar
Cover picture of Binayak Sen courtesy: www.binayaksen.net

RAJPAL & SONS, Kashmere Gate, Delhi-110 006
website: www.rajpalpublishing.com
e-mail: mail@rajpalpublishing.com

CONTENTS

FOREWORD

Initially when Minnie Vaid spoke to us in the autumn of 2009 and said she was doing this book, I had mixed feelings. Part of me, desperately seeking privacy as I coped with cancer therapy, didn't really want to get involved with the story that Minnie was trying to tell. At another level was the creeping concern that had haunted me for the two years preceding: How were we (and Minnie now!) going to make sense of what had happened to Binayak and to us—as a struggle following upon a misfortune that was purely personal, or as one that, while bringing intense personal pain, only made sense in the context of whatever was happening to people in our beloved Chhattisgarh? As someone who teaches Women's Studies, the central concern came back again and again to the relationship between the personal and the political.

I am glad to say, from discussions with Minnie, that one could not have coped with the intermeshing of the personal and the political any better than she did—the range and depth of the developmental crisis in our land, the militarization and forced displacement faced by so many men, women and children, and the background thread of our family's struggle against Binayak's unjust detention by the state of Chhattisgarh. As we have interacted over the last year, I have again and again been impressed by her fierce commitment to the truth, her relentless search for the sources, and her high professional and ethical integrity.

The campaign to free Dr Binayak Sen was unique in its involvement of civil society and individuals as well as human rights organizations across the country and beyond. From the time of his original detention on May 14, 2007 when a group of his friends and well wishers as well as people in the human rights and civil liberties movement began the protests and representations, the campaign gathered mass and was a huge international uproar by the time he was actually released. It is difficult for me even now to write about this, as it was humanly impossible to keep track of a campaign that was so widely dispersed in nature. There are so many details that I still do not have, and I am afraid that I will inadvertently leave someone or the other out of our list of acknowledgements! So many people who worked quietly for his release and to set the record straight about him, chose to work incognito and did not pursue public credit. The issue of Binayak's detention, to everyone's credit, was never taken up in isolation, but always in the context of large scale human rights violations and militarization in Chhattisgarh. The highlights as I remember are:

o Protests and protest meetings in Delhi, Kolkata, Chennai, Coimbatore and other cities by human rights groups like the PUCL, PUDR and APDR.

o The involvement of the Christian Medical College alumni, nationally as well as in the UK and the USA. These friends wrote hundreds of letters, petitions, as well as lobbied with whoever they thought was able to influence the authorities.

o The Mumbai Committee for the release of Binayak Sen, which organized press conferences, rallies and events in various places in Mumbai, particularly during the second year.

o The Delhi Committee for the release of Binayak Sen, which made similar efforts, and organized two concerts on the lawns of Rabindra Bhawan on May 14, 2008, and May 14, 2009, to mark the first and second anniversaries of arrest, at which many artistes and cultural workers took part.

o The efforts of the group 'Doctors in Defence of Dr Binayak Sen' who drew attention to his work in the area of community health through their publication "Indian Doctor in Jail: The Story of Dr Binayak Sen."

o Amnesty International which organized an international letter-writing campaign through which Binayak in jail received thousands of letters of support, and the authorities in Chhattisgarh received letters of which we have no direct information. Amnesty also adopted Binayak as a prisoner of conscience, and dedicated a large part of its efforts at the Edinburgh festival to the issue of Binayak and what was happening in Chhattisgarh.

o Other international networks like the Human Rights Watch, the Association for India's Development, and the Asian Centre for Human Rights also raised the issue at different times through their reports.

o The Raipur rally which began in March 2009 and went on till May 2009, during which on every Monday there were groups of people from across the country who courted arrest at Raipur, demanding that Binayak be released. While the first few groups numbered around fifty, the numbers swelled to over 150 in the later rounds, and had participants from places as far as Karnataka, Kashmir and Gujarat.

o Academic organizations like the Indian Academy of Social Sciences and the Global Health Council which bestowed on Binayak the RR Keithan and Jonathan Mann awards, respectively during 2007-08 in recognition of his work as well as in solidarity.

I remember today the many people whose lives and work influenced the decisions Binayak took about his own life and career options. Many of these influences are described in the book that we have on our hands, but there is one heritage that I feel I must specially recall. Dr A K Sen of Patna, my uncle, (husband of my *phulmashima*) was at once a great doctor, great communist, and a great human being. His fame as a doctor, and particularly as a doctor who cared for the poor, was phenomenal, and spread way beyond Patna city. Patients came to him from across the Ganga, and touts roamed the ghats to lure patients away into the clutches of other, less scrupulous commercial doctors. The number of people he looked after only out of his genuine concern are legion. Recently I read a reminiscence from the RJD MP Jabir Hussain that described how a mother from one of Patna's *jhuggies*, whose son had been saved by *meshomoshai* after a night long vigil at his own home, observed his death anniversary with flowers and candles.

Meshomoshai always referred to Binayak as his favourite son in law, and the two had an obvious common wavelength when they met. When I read the police chargesheet on Binayak proclaiming his apparent lack of income from his medical practice as evidence of his seditious politics, I could have laughed. I wonder what the police would have made of *meshomoshai's* super extended guest list. Like many of *meshomoshai's* patients, Binayak's patients almost never had anything to pay, and often stayed over for dinner and a night's stay for observation. Yet as we saw during the Raipur rally, the number of patients—men, women and children from the working class *bastis* of Dalli Rajhara, Bhilai and Urla—who had stories to tell about Dr Binayak Sen were so many. A supporter from Pune who was changing trains at Nagpur while coming to Raipur for a rally in support of Binayak, mentioned casually to a fruit seller where he was headed and why. The fruit seller, the son of a striking worker from Bhilai, wanted to know if this was Dr Binayak Sen that they were talking about, and offered a hundred rupee note to the concerned person to hand over to me towards legal expenses for Binayak's case.

In many ways what has been hardest has been the deliberate and malicious vilification of Binayak by the Chhattisgarh police and the ever so obliging media. The gloating news bylines in the Raipur press describing Binayak as a Naxal *dakiya*, a Maoist mastermind whom the police were looking for since a long time, the misplaced quotes from neighbours saying that their home was always being visited by young men and women who stayed for long hours and "obviously ate there as well", long time associates refusing even to recognize me or my daughters...this is the stuff that my nightmares are now made up of. I know I should feel only pity for the backward consciousness of some, but this will still take me some time.

Binayak and I came together fairly early in our lives, and in many ways grew together intellectually and personally. It is a very precious bonding, and yet we have also retained our separate interests, preferences, and persona. This has always appeared to be difficult to understand for some people who are more used to dealing in binaries and find it easier to grapple with a situation in which one or the other partner is dominating the relationship. After all these years and our many differences, he is a person I still respect. Life with him has not always been easy. However, it has always been interesting and has always challenged me to stretch the limits. I cannot imagine living any other way.

Raipur   –Ilina Sen

LETTER FROM 22 NOBEL LAUREATES

May 9, 2008

Her Excellency Mrs. Pratibha Patil, *President*
His Excellency Dr. Manmohan Singh, *Prime Minister*
His Excellency Mr. Hans Raj Bhardwaj, *Minister of Law and Justice*
His Excellency Mr. E S L Narsimhan, *Governor of Chhattisgarh*
The Honourable Dr. Raman Singh, *Chief Minister, Chhattisgarh*
The Honourable Mr. Ramvichar Netam, *Home Minister, Chhattisgarh*
The Honourable Mr. Shivraj Singh, *Chief Secretary, Chhattisgarh*

We, the undersigned Nobel Laureates, congratulate you on the prestigious international honour that will be bestowed for the first time on a citizen of India. As you are no doubt aware, the Global Health Council (GHC), the world's largest membership alliance of public health organizations and professionals, has selected Dr. Binayak Sen of Raipur, Chhattisgarh to be the recipient of the 2008 Jonathan Mann Award for Global Health and Human Rights. We write to request that Dr. Sen be enabled to receive the award in person at the GHC's Annual Conference in Washington, D.C. on May 29, 2008. We also wish to express grave concern that Dr. Sen appears to be incarcerated solely for peacefully exercising his fundamental human rights, in contravention of Articles 19 (freedom of opinion and expression) and 22 (freedom of association) of the International Covenant on Civil and Political Rights—to which India is a state party—and that he is charged under two internal security laws that do not comport with international human rights standards. We are pleased to learn that Dr. Sen's trial has, after numerous delays, now begun. While the judicial process involving our professional colleague moves forward, we respectfully request that Dr. Sen be freed from incarceration on humanitarian grounds to receive his award and to continue his important medical work.

Yours sincerely

Peter Agre, *Chemistry 2003*
Kenneth J. Arrow, *Economics 1972*
Claude Cohen-Tannoudji, *Physics 1997*
Robert Curl, *Chemistry 1996*
Johann Deisenhofer, *Chemistry 1988*
Paul Greengard, *Medicine 2000*
Roger Guillemin, *Medicine 1977*
Francois Jacob, *Medicine 1965*
Eric Kandel, *Medicine 2000*
Sir Harold Kroto, *Chemistry 1996*
Finn Kydland, *Economics 2004*
Yuan T. Lee, *Chemistry 1986*
Craig C. Mello, *Medicine 2006*
John Polanyi, *Chemistry 1986*
Richard J. Roberts, *Medicine 1993*
F. Sherwood Rowland, *Chemistry 1995*
Jens C. Skou, *Chemistry 1997*
Phillip A. Sharp, *Medicine 1993*
Charles Townes, *Physics 1964*
Harold Varmus, *Medicine 1989*
Sir John E. Walker, *Chemistry 1997*
Torsten Wiesel, *Medicine 1981*

ACKNOWLEDGEMENTS

This is possibly the most gratifying part of writing this book, perhaps because it seems to be one of the most anticipated pages as far as my family and friends are concerned! I had to actually ask them if this would be the only page they would read and was only partially reassured by their nodding smiles. So here goes:

My thanks to the first person who read the first paragraph of the first chapter and suggested a minor change, my 17 year old niece, Ridhi.

Robust thanks also to my 14 year old nephew Rishabh who wanted the book to be dedicated to him for his invaluable moral support (and it certainly was!) during all the times I went home to write in Pune.

Grateful thanks to the only two people who consistently read each chapter and provided insightful feedback, my "critics" as I called them, Sherna Gandhy and Unni Vijayan. They minced no words, telling it like it is, yet nudging me along right till the last chapter. Without their comments I might still be trudging away...

Researcher Neha Belvalkar helped with collation of data.

Needless to add, without the continuous help of the Sen family and their numerous friends all over the country and especially the state of Chhattisgarh, this book could not have been written. My sincere thanks to each and every one of them.

Of the editor-publisher duo it is hard for me not to appear gushing, for the first was hearteningly encouraging and the second stood by me for the duration like a rock, unforgettable women both.

And finally, gratitude from the bottom of my heart for the one person who coped with the daily grind and grumbles, angst and agony that accompanies the writing of a first book—someone I call "Paal Paysam".

PROLOGUE

The very first meeting was slightly disappointing though I would not admit it, even to myself.

I blamed it on my own inflated expectations.

I first saw Binayak Sen or rather a file photograph of him on the pages of "Outlook" magazine in its May 26, 2008 issue, the headline boldly proclaiming: "Framed, Nailed, Hanged". The article was very well-written, the story engrossing, the man himself awe-inspiring.

I can vividly recall my reaction as I finished reading the chilling account of an accomplished doctor who had worked in rural health care for almost three decades, having spent a whole year in jail for speaking out against human rights abuses in Chhattisgarh.

I was working as a creative producer for a corporate house in those days and reading about Binayak Sen in jail, with a chargesheet that called him a "fake" doctor, I wanted to leave the confined space of that office and make a documentary film on the subject.

Documentaries were what I did for a living in any case, and health care in rural India, injustice, human rights, a defender to defend— this was a familiar world, my world. A world I had entered, reported and presented to television audiences in the country for over fifteen years through rural short films and documentaries.

In fact, the very first episode of "Roots", a television non-fiction show I produced and directed in the nineties, featured Primary Health Centres (PHC) in remote rural Rajasthan where doctors were a rarity rather than the rule and "Health for all by 2000" just an empty slogan.

More recently, I had been similarly inspired to make a documentary film on Kanpur IIT engineer Satyendra Dubey, widely believed to have been killed for blowing the whistle and exposing corruption during his stint at the government's National Highway Authority of India's (NHAI) Golden Quadrilateral project. Another courageous man making a courageous choice, forsaking easier options.

I have always been intrigued by such people, such choices, such single-minded determination to achieve tasks that most people consider unviable or not worth the effort.

For me, therefore, a person like Binayak Sen who voluntarily worked among villagers most of his life and also had the courage of his convictions would have been compelling much before I met him or read his shocking story.

I continued to track the Binayak Sen story in the media (mostly print media with a rare television report) for almost a year, became part of the Free Binayak Sen campaign on Facebook and then finally decided to take leave from that corporate office and walk alongside more than 600 supporters in the May 14, 2009 Raipur rally demanding his release from Raipur Central Jail.

In the 43 degree heat and dust of a sweltering rally, marching in orderly, double-file rows with activists, tribals, trade union workers, doctors, villagers, health workers, students, the single most overwhelming thought in my mind was, I am back to *my* roots, again, thank God.

Binayak Sen was granted bail on May 25, 2009. He was fifty-nine years old at that time.

Just two months later as I walked up the stairs to his modest second-floor flat at A-26, Surya Apartments in Raipur, I really didn't know what to expect.

Map of Chhattisgarh

Chapter One

A Reluctant Hero

Raipur

I am merely aware of a slight breathlessness, an anticipatory excitement that refuses to go away.

In two years, Binayak Sen has acquired iconic status. Everyone wants to meet him, talk to him, touch him, almost as if by doing so, some of his "heroic-ness" will rub off on them.

The door opens (it has the famous Free Binayak Sen poster of a bearded, smiling Binayak-behind-bars pasted on the left side) and I step inside for a brief five-minute wait.

I scan the room, divided into two sections. The right corner is clearly the designated social area with chairs, a small table and bookshelves. The left side looks more official with a computer, more books and papers strewn around. The overall effect is clearly confining.

A moment later that feeling changes as a sari-clad Ilina Sen enters, smiling, warm—she is someone I have met before, during the May rally, a strong, courageous person.

She introduces me to her husband Binayak.

Green kurta-white pyjama, dark rings under hooded eyes, hair slightly ruffled, no beard, a quiet, almost stern demeanour.

A firm handshake that stays with you.

He does not speak at all after Ilina completes her introduction of me in her customary gentle and friendly manner. Instead he listens carefully, even as I take up the tale and continue the condensed version of my life story (the professional part of course).

This is in fact, as you later realize, a trademark trait. Binayak will hear you out without interrupting till you are almost reduced to making inane comments to fill the silences. After almost ten minutes of unbroken silence, I am forced to resort to showing him the DVD of a promo I had shot of the May 14 Raipur rally, just to break both the silence and the ice.

After a few false starts on the computer, the DVD begins, resplendent with exuberant dances, songs, protest performances, slogan shouting, organized marching, ending with his own image and voice appealing for support for civil liberties.

Binayak watches the four-minute promo with intense concentration, asks Ilina who the cultural performers are, and seems a bit taken aback at the sheer volume of support, the number of people captured on camera in the promo. He watches the end credits carefully, does not comment at all, just moves to the right side of the room and sits down.

I allow myself a small twinge of disappointment.

But I can sense a slight unbending...as I start telling him about the combined book and documentary film project I have taken on, based on his life and life choices. I tell him that I have chosen to quit my job to do so.

He addresses me for the first time, choosing his words carefully. Many meetings later, this too becomes a familiar, recognizable trait. "I am very grateful to you, first of all, for all your support. I am very conscious of the fact that there has been a huge popular upsurge of opinion supporting me...I don't believe it's because of my personal qualities. I am the same person I was two years ago, before I was imprisoned, I have been quietly working for twenty eight years. I am quite happy being that person, quite happy that nobody knew about me."

"But now many, many people want to know about you sir..."

"Please don't call me sir..." he laughs and interrupts, waving his hands.

"I guess it will take me some time, I have been reading about you for more than a year, following your case, and it's a bit overwhelming for me to even just sit in front of you right now," I reply frankly.

I then tell him the basic motivation behind the dual project, encapsulated in the one-liner summarizing the promo for the film: What kind of man elicits such unprecedented support from such diverse types of people, from such varied walks of life?

Binayak is thoughtful and tells me that he really wants to know the answer to that question himself. He suggests I ask it from a wider historical perspective rather than assessing him or his personal qualities.

"But don't people admire those who have the courage of their convictions, who do what they perhaps wanted to do but could not...?" I offer hesitantly.

Ilina interrupts to add decisively, "It also depends on the circumstances you are faced with. Sometimes you have situations thrust upon you, and you just have to deal with them. No one is born thinking he is going to become a great person."

Binayak nods in agreement.

The Sens have a prior engagement so I take their leave, asking for time later.

"That's your prerogative," says Binayak. "We just need to adjust our timings. Stay with us tomorrow evening, we can chat till late at night."

And with that, my much-anticipated meeting is over.

~

Sitting in a cycle rickshaw, still the preferred and common means of transport in Raipur, weaving through small lanes and bylanes, I try to shrug aside the slight feeling of anti-climax, first through denial.

I call up close friends who have also been part of the Binayak story either as supporters or sympathetic observers or merely because I have talked to them about Binayak so much for more than a year! I tell them what a wonderful experience it was...meeting Binayak Sen for the first time. They respond with appropriate expressions of envy or delight at the achievement of a much desired goal.

Then I look inward at my slight disappointment. I had attributed larger-than-life dimensions of an almost heroic nature to Binayak Sen and expected him to conform to that image in my mind. That didn't happen.

I reason with myself that what drives me to explore Binayak's life, his choices, his trials is not the fact that he is considered a hero by so many people but the kind of life he seems to have led, which I want to know more about.

Then I turn around and question my own beliefs about how a hero should appear to others. Are there certain qualities that dictate the behaviour, accessibility, aura of a hero?

Why should an intensely private person open his doors and himself to anyone who wants to know more about him after his newly-found celebrity status? What defines a hero and why are people so attracted to heroes? Why are people in this country particularly so addicted to the need for a hero?

Binayak Sen is undoubtedly a hero for many people today, albeit an unlikely one. He certainly does not fit the stereotype and in many ways can be considered a throwback to the good old days...when people like Jayaprakash Narayan were heroes.

In an era where fighting injustice mattered.

Speaking up for the truth mattered.

Ideals and principles mattered.

Binayak Sen has done all this in a different era, and incredibly, it does seem to have mattered, to a whole lot of people. In 2007, only a select few would have known who Binayak Sen was, much less about the work he was doing but just two years later—the day before I first met Binayak Sen—I googled his name on the internet (out of sheer curiosity) and got 56,200 results in 0.38 seconds. On Facebook where supporters ran an extremely successful and relentless Free Binayak Sen campaign, the most unlikely people whose daily lives were not and would never be touched by Binayak's concerns asked "Who is Binayak Sen and why is he in jail?" "What is the Salwa Judum?"

For the two years and eleven days that Binayak was in jail, from May 14, 2007 to May 25, 2009, there were people outside jail who made sure that he was not forgotten, not alone, not silenced.

The media, strangely enough, remained silent for the most part, almost completely for the first year and then sporadically, the national mainstream media began covering the story as events unfolded in the case. A few magazines like "Tehelka", newspapers like "The Hindu" and some television news channels profiled

Binayak's work as well. The regional media either demonized him with a vengeance with one-sided, partisan reporting or didn't report his news at all. Binayak Sen was not "breaking news" material till he was released on bail, after which he was feted by news channels en masse, asking him how he "felt about his release".

What was continuous and sustained, however, was the people's support for him, which later came to be described as a movement, gathering momentum and more supporters on the way, culminating in the glad tidings of his release. Who were all these people and why did they come out in such numbers to make sure Binayak Sen did not meet the fate that hundreds, indeed thousands, of such detenues face in India's jails? Was it a sense of outrage, of injustice that motivated this reaction, that a man who had spent almost thirty years working in rural health care should be incarcerated for following his conscience? Or for speaking out against the state-sponsored counter-insurgency vigilante operation called Salwa Judum and its many human rights excesses, where very few would have had the courage to do so?

~

I climb the stairs to A-26 once again the next evening in search of answers.

Binayak answers the door himself, greets me, goes into the kitchen to fetch water from an old-fashioned *surahi*. The dark circles under his eyes seem more pronounced. He also looks more tired and it is, after all, almost the end of the day, 8 pm.

People come and go at intervals, another accepted ritual in this household. I recognize some faces from the May 14 rally—trade unionist Sudha Bhardwaj, Dr Yogesh Jain from Ganyari's Jan Swasthya Sahyog who leave as I enter. Others, like media professor Kripashanker Chaubey sit around and chat until the official interview begins.

We tell Binayak about the festive atmosphere across cities the day he got bail. Chaubeyji talks about the live coverage on Kolkata TV, channels carrying the news in Orissa, in Kerala, in other states. I describe in turn how people called each other up, conveying congratulations, "*Badhai ho…aapko bhi*" was the common refrain. It seemed like a day of personal victory for so many. A day of jubilation.

Binayak listens, still silent, still absorbing the extent and aftermath of a celebrity status that seems not to sit easy on his now-lean shoulders. Looking at him, I remember Ilina worriedly telling me in May that he had lost 20 kg in jail. He appears preoccupied, even troubled.

I decide to ask him directly, "People think of you as a hero, an icon, want to touch you, want to be a part of you, be a part of your struggle. How does all of this sit with you, you seem to be a bit uncomfortable with it…"

His answer is emphatic. "There is no question of being a hero, we are at a parti]cular historical juncture and large populations are involved in that—individuals do not make history. We have to work our way through the problems with which we are confronted and the idea of a hero or an icon wouldn't really be helpful in deciding what path to take."

At the same time Binayak respects the way people feel about him. He agrees there were grounds for their outrage because his spending two years in jail was definitely a miscarriage of justice besides which the government was trying to present a biased analysis of events and the public was angry at being taken for a ride. So their sense of righteousness was aroused and when, eventually he was granted bail and came out of jail, the public found some sort of catharsis and attributed personal glory to him.

But at the same time, there is so much more that is going on today, warns Binayak. We need to understand the situation, the kind of sequestration of natural resources that is going on—land, river resources, privatization of water through dams. We are at a bad point in history and we need to collectively understand and change this.

The words are measured carefully before being uttered, they gain weight as they are spoken, the thought processes, the ideology they reflect all tend to intimidate you a little, make you feel a little out of your depth. Sometimes a simple question will be answered analytically at a much higher level.

Since this is only my second meeting with him, I have no understanding yet as to why Binayak is so determinedly opposed to both accepting the label of a hero and the *idea* of the label itself. It isn't that I want to force the tag on him either, but public perception and expectation propel me to continue.

So I probe further. "People who see you as a hero today, or for the last two years, are now also aware of your achievements over the last twenty eight years, people who have never seen a rural health clinic and had no reason really to place you on a pedestal, which they now do."

And once again, the denial is swift, not self-deprecatory or falsely modest but a decisive non-acceptance of what I am putting forth as a possibility for the following he commands today.

Binayak will not take on roles or mantles that he does not believe in.

"My work has always been as part of a team...the term 'hero' implies some kind of individual achievement. If I represent, and I really don't know what it is that I am supposed to represent, but if it is the cause of the people then yes, I share it with all my colleagues," he informs me.

He works with large numbers of people, he says quietly, who are all dedicated to the cause, people working in very bad circumstances for a particular process (of change, of transformation) to take place for the people of our country—a very large number of whom are also in a very bad way. Being part of that process that will change the lives of those millions of our countrymen is Binayak's only claim, but not as an individual. "My name has become prominent due to particular reasons at a certain point in time but I am no exception and I take strength in the fact that I am no exception," he says.

I remind him once again of the double-barrelled reason for the iconic status...public perception of his unjust arrest, his long jail term, and the relentless campaign to free him that extended even outside the country.

Binayak laughs a little, then says firmly and gently, "I am just a very ordinary man, working along particular lines, especially for human rights. I am part of a large group of dedicated people who have been working for many years...that is my strength and that is my identity. My strength is not riding into the sunset. There is a widespread sense of outrage today at the times in which we are living and people are not able to visualize a way out of this, so when they see someone or a group that is actually working, I think people do feel a sense of sympathy, not in a sense of pity but fellow feeling...I am very glad to claim that but not in any individual capacity."

"There were writers, film directors, intellectuals, actors...who supported your campaign..." I interject.

Binayak ponders, "Well, I understand that...no...actually I don't understand that. I really don't know how I got from jail into this kind of a conformation, but as the focus of widespread outrage that people are feeling across the country and the world...if I am the focus of some small victory against the forces of oppression, then I do claim that gladly."

He talks with wonder about people like film maker Aparna Sen whose support was "fantastic" and others like Shaoli Mitra who he says he grew up hero-worshipping. They all spoke up for him, he seems unable to digest all of this.

We speak of mutual friends who worked on the poster that went on to become a hallmark, reprinted on T-shirts, campaign logos, leaflets, signature campaigns...he is just a bit overcome at hearing this. "So many different people put different skills to different uses for me, I didn't even know, I am grateful..." It isn't something he takes for granted at all.

His elder daughter Pranhita, a Mass Communications graduate from Xaviers, Mumbai, who also took part in the May 14 rally and had earlier told me how she too wanted to make a film on her father, enters the flat with characteristic boisterousness. Her "Baba" hugs her affectionately and we break for dinner which is laid out in one of the bedrooms.

It is a simple meal and Binayak is an attentive host. Ilina's mother is also present, visiting the family. My mobile phone rings for just two beats and Binayak recognizes the haunting tune from the film "Sholay" instantly. I ask him if he is fond of Hindi movies. Courtesy Pranhita's ambitions of being a cinematographer, they all watch films these days, he says with a smile.

And slowly, bit by bit, seeing that smile, seeing him hug his daughter, attend to my meal solicitously, my first impressions of him being stern and unapproachable start to crumble and fade away.

After the meal, everyone disperses and Binayak and I continue our conversation though he is visibly tired. But this is the only time he has during this visit and he has things to say and I have questions I need answers to if I want to tell the Binayak

Sen story the way it deserves to be told.

What is unique about this story?

It is basically a story that leads you to hope that things will happen because good people doing good work still exist.

And it is probably out of the need that people have to look up to someone doing that work that the Free Binayak campaign arose, culminating in the unifying feelings of elation and vindication on the day of his release on bail.

Binayak fulfilled that need without saying a word. He was, after all, in jail for all of that time. Today when he *is* at liberty to speak, he is wary of this "heroism" turning counter-productive if it draws people's attention away from the problems that need to be addressed.

He outlines his thoughts, carefully weighing his words, "We cannot allow ourselves to move away from the forces of history because heroes are not going to change the course of history. In India we now have a system where there is really a rapacious process of sequestration of resources into private hands or the elite, however you like to characterize it, and the poor are getting poorer. The government's own figures tell us that a vast majority of our countrymen are living lives of deprivation. I prefer the word deprivation to poverty because the word poverty suggests that it seems to have just happened by itself.

Deprivation is an active process and poverty is not a default option (his voice rises forcefully). There is an actual discipline and energy and diligence being devoted to creating the poverty that we see, so we really need to make this deprivation the target of our joint efforts and if, in the process, we have some victories and if some individuals are associated with those victories and we celebrate the victories by invoking the names of those individuals that's okay, but it should not move us away from the realization of the fundamental processes at work."

I ask him if that means he will go back and resume his work quietly once the trial and its attendant hoopla and hype are over and turn his back on the status he has acquired over the last two years.

His denial is immediate, "No, no, I don't think this is something we can just leave behind like a suitcase left behind at a railway station. I think this huge national and international campaign *does* have significance, we have to try and read that significance, take that process forward towards the broader goals we have set for ourselves as a collective, capitalize on our gains...to the extent that we have a victory, not just in the sense that I was in jail and now I am out of jail but that this whole process came to a particular focus and had its way with the forces which were trying to keep it constrained, so that is something worth celebrating and we need to give it its proper due and also use it as a resource for work."

For a person who has been freed only two months ago, facing a trial with no clear time frame for its resolution, and confronting unwelcome and enormous disruption in his professional and personal life, Binayak Sen is nevertheless a man with a larger plan. A plan that will build on the equity and fame and the "greatness" that he is so unwilling to accept but that has been thrust upon him by his many admirers. A plan for working towards justice and peace for the future.

Once again, he warns against unrealistic expectations of any Messiah-like deliverance or intervention on his part when I suggest that people may want more than him just building on the support that he has received so far. "I hope that I and the Free Binayak movement...of course I have not been involved, I have only been the subject of the movement, I hope they will not fall into the misleading traps that will render not only ineffective but be harmful for the overall movement of the people. Having said that, my aim is to try and build a constituency for peace along with equity and justice and in this effort, we will appeal to people across the country to build up a momentum for peace that is so strong that the military stress of the government or the military response from the Maoists will be put aside as a result of the sound of the thousands of voices raised together."

His tone is heartfelt and the words acquire prophetic proportions. I forget the small divided section of the space we are sitting in, imagining instead the visual picture he has just created in my mind.

The discussion continues back and forth, my questioning how exactly he is planning to pursue a course of action that is even wider in scope than his earlier work that got him into such trouble, given that the key players are still the same, the institutions are still the same and his reply is that there are no easy solutions and hopefully the suffering of the people in the cause of peace will be more fruitful than those who are victims of war.

He emphasizes that these are hopes, not guarantees but that the issue of peace, equity and justice needs to be evoked with the same energy and dedication that other approaches have generated.

It is now more than two hours since we started the interview with the concept of a hero, people's need to gravitate towards a hero in today's troubled times, and Binayak appearing to be a reluctant hero. He has taken just one break, stopping mid-sentence to gather his thoughts, running his hands through his already mussed hair, pacing the small corridor for a while before sitting down and completing his analysis. He is particular about what gets recorded, about how his sequence of thoughts and therefore his comments will be perceived, changing words and phrases till they sit right.

I decide to end the session by asking him the all important question about choices. This is, after all, the crux of the Binayak

Sen story, the choices he made and the price he paid for making them.

I start a bit hesitantly, apprehensive that he may take offence, "Do you think the choices you made in your life have been difficult ones...after graduation from Christian Medical College, Vellore, you could have gone abroad, started a lucrative private practice, but you chose to practice medicine in villages. Then later you could have kept quiet about the human rights abuses but you didn't, so you came to the government's notice and were jailed. You always took a stand that was difficult, so in a sense is it true that you had to *defend* your choices rather than *celebrate* them?"

He takes a long time to answer, characteristically as I am now beginning to recognize. "I don't believe in self-sacrifice. Everyone lives their lives according to certain principles. I do so too and I take decisions based on those principles. Certainly if you look at it from a conventional viewpoint, many people within our group, especially family, have paid a heavy price for whatever has been done. But the decisions were made on the basis of principles established long before, they didn't arise at the point of decision. So it's not that we take a decision that is difficult as opposed to one that is easy, at the point of the decision. It doesn't happen that way. We have chosen to live as a part of groups, as part of organizations, that is our great privilege and we believe that is a better way to live, a better way for *us* to live.

"Ivan Illich used a word which is very important to me, convivial, not in the sense of laughing etc. but convivial in the sense of living together. That principle of conviviality you can't characterize as being difficult or self-sacrificing. That was the way we had to go."

I am intrigued and say so. "That's a very interesting and unique insight, as almost every media article about you talks of how you could have done so many things but gave it all up to do *jan-kalyan* (social service) in the villages."

Binayak's face lights up with a rare smile, it changes his face dramatically, making him look younger and suddenly carefree, "We have just one life to lead so you might as well live it in the way that you have the most fun."

It is the one sentence and philosophy that resonates so perfectly with my frame of mind at that moment, having given up a stifling job that I hated, that I end up agreeing heartily with him and *now* the ice is well and truly broken.

He talks of all the people who have participated with him through the process, of how they too feel the same way, that whatever the price they had to pay, however difficult some of the times were, the opportunities of work they all shared have been a great privilege. And that they had a lot of fun doing the work they did!

I tell him that I want to re-trace that journey, find those friends, share their stories and in that convivial sharing, find a Binayak Sen story to share with the world. I ask for a list of names; of friends, co-workers and colleagues who know him well, who can piece together the different parts of his life, his work, his personality so that I can discover the Binayak Sen *they* know. And let *them* tell the stories…

He looks at me quizzically for a while and then gives me the names and places, enunciating them carefully, watching me write it all down. As yet of course, they mean nothing to me but these names will take on a different light very soon and I can hardly wait.

The next morning heralds the first day of my journey and at 6 am, Binayak is the only one awake in his home. He makes filter coffee for the two of us, we drink it in near total, companionable silence and it is soon time for me to go to Bilaspur to meet Sudha Bhardwaj.

She is the first person on my list.

Bilaspur, Ganyari, Dalli Rajhara, Vellore, Bagrumnala, Dantewada... the names hold a peculiar fascination of their own. They are the key to my search for the Binayak Sen story.

Chapter Two

THE HEADY DAYS

Dalli Rajhara

The noisy autorickshaw rattles through the dusty and crowded streets of Bilaspur town and deposits me at Nehru Nagar near the Hanuman Mandir as per specifications, where I start my search for D-8, the residence of feisty advocate Sudha Bhardwaj.

She is the slogan-shouting, extremely articulate, trade unionist Chhattisgarh Mukti Morcha (CMM) activist-lawyer who enthused the crowds with her vigorous appeals at the May 14, 2009 rally for Binayak Sen.

Despite her detailed directions I cannot find her house and start asking various shopkeepers around the area. Finally one of them points upwards to a rather dilapidated building.

I climb the stairs to the first floor and discover that Sudha actually lives in a room in a *chawl*. Right now, her door is locked. I wait outside patiently, her friendly neighbour invites me in, offers water and tea. Twenty minutes later the sound of scampering feet running up prompts the neighbour to say, "*unki beti aa gayi hai toh who bhi aati hongi.*"

Sudha Bhardwaj enters, trademark cotton sari, a bit crumpled already at just 10 am, beads of perspiration on her forehead. She is hot and bothered since the house lock has to be broken as the keys are misplaced.

Her dimpled, impish thirteen-year-old daughter Anusuya watches me curiously. She is then asked to run off to buy cold drinks once we enter the one-room home.

Sunlight filters in through just the one, single-barred window next to the door where a desk and two chairs facing each other complete the essential furniture. I see a computer and heavy tomes of law books lining bookshelves from floor to almost the ceiling, dust gathering on most of them.

Having travelled since 6.30 am, I ask to freshen up. The bathroom is just beyond a little alcove that serves as a kitchen. A large earthen pot filled with water stands in one corner. The toilet is Indian-style as is the norm here, the latch on the door made of iron rings that fit the holder. This one-room house, the things in it, the starkness and the simplicity are like a punch in the stomach even as the true meaning of the phrase "walk the talk" comes home to me.

Having also washed up and taken a moment to breathe, Sudha apologizes for the wait. The resignation in her tone suggests this is a daily affair, and she does indeed lead an incredibly hectic life. When you hear her rather deep-timbred voice, you can't help thinking that this is a voice of a person who has done her fair share of slogan-shouting and speeches.

Currently, as a criminal lawyer at the High Court of Chhattisgarh based in Bilaspur, she represents some of the rape victims of the infamous Salwa Judum while also helping various people's organizations, NGOs (Non Government Organization) and trade unions with their legal issues.

As we settle down to talk about Binayak Sen whom she has known closely for more than twenty-three years, it strikes me rather forcefully that the forty-seven-year-old Sudha could well be the next Binayak Sen.

In fact, she already is. Not the next but *another* Binayak Sen, courageous, standing up for the rights of the underprivileged, working amongst them as one of their own, uncaring of personal consequences.

Her own story is equally fascinating. Sudha was a child prodigy, topping her classes, going on to do a five-year integrated Masters in Mathematics from the Indian Institute of Technology, Kanpur, passing out in 1984 with excellent grades and the prospect of a great career and future ahead. She also had an American passport courtesy her birth in that country (her parents—both economists— had at one time done research at the Massachusetts Institute of Technology.) She chose to give up her American passport and the life that would have accompanied it and instead took up volunteer work with a trade union. This trade union was the CMM and its leader was a man called Shankar Guha Niyogi.

Niyogi was an inspirational figure for both Sudha and Binayak. He was the founder of the CMM, a labour union movement that he successfully helmed for fourteen years from 1977 till he was assassinated on September 28,1991. He was also hailed as a social thinker of the alternative development movement, a mass movement for genuine change, which was clearly an appealing proposition for people like Binayak and Sudha.

~

Sudha begins describing those early days with a nostalgic smile. "I and most of my comrades in the CMM refer to Binayak Sen as Doctor Saab. That's because it was a working class culture, it was a trade union, but when we say Doc Saab we don't mean to place him on a higher level at all because Saab is the antithesis of what he is. A more compassionate person than him will be hard to find in this world. He hates inequality; he can't bear it. For instance he wouldn't be able to bear someone sitting on the floor if you're sitting on a chair, he finds it repulsive, that's the kind of person he is. The Doc Saab label was just out of habit."

Her earliest memories of "Doc Saab" are of him carrying baby Pranhita on his back. He was very supportive of his wife Ilina, and Sudha considers the couple a role model. "One incident I still clearly remember was in Shaheed Hospital (founded and run by the workers themselves in Dalli Rajhara) when a baby being weighed was crying a lot and Binayak picked it up and it quietened down immediately. He had a way of communicating without language and he is really good with children. I always felt paediatrics must be so difficult since a child cannot tell you what is wrong, but he was really sensitive. For such a very compassionate person to respond to brutalities and atrocities…it was very painful for him, the anti-thesis of his character…" Her voice trails off.

She mentions agitations and struggles that Binayak participated in, in that era—the Rajnandgaon BMC textile mill negotiation (July-December 1984), and the *Kabir Panthi mutth* where the *mahant* had seized a lot of land and the CMM under Niyogi was spearheading a protest. "Binayak was very active in all these struggles, he always tried to look at it in all its aspects, holistically. He was also very encouraging towards the women *karyakartas*, or workers. That was very typical of him," adds Sudha.

And then, she says, there was a gap…Binayak and Ilina left Shaheed Hospital to work outside Dalli Rajhara on various fronts, while she stayed on with the CMM. Since her union work involved liaising with lawyers, she decided to become one herself, clearing the Bar exams in 2000.

Sudha's favourite Binayak Sen story is of a more recent time. "When Doc Saab was in jail, a group of doctors from Pune and Mumbai were visiting Bastar as part of a fact-finding team. En route they stopped to buy bananas from a wayside stall. They were talking about going to Raipur later and about meeting Dr Sen. The banana-seller asked them if they were talking about Binayak Sen. When they said yes they were, he fished out a hundred rupee note from his pocket and said, 'You must be needing a lot of money to fight his case, isn't it? I'm a worker he had treated, will you please give this to him?' He inspired that kind of feeling, so many people supported him," she says, her eyes shining.

She lists the numerous groups of peasants, workers, trade unionists, contract workers from Bhilai, Raipur, Raigarh, villagers and tribals from Dhamtari and Bagrumnala who all came out in each rally to protest against the doctor's imprisonment—voiceless people who came forward bravely and spoke out in his favour.

"After his arrest, the police raided his clinic illegally, looked at all the records, tore off some of the posters, surrounded the villages where he had been working and tried to scare the villagers by saying he was a Naxalite. Almost all of them bravely replied, 'We don't know what he is to you, *saheb. Hamare liye toh woh Bhagwan hain.* For us he is a god. He has saved us from many things.' "

She talks of jail visits when she would ask him how he was. "*Doc Saab aap kaise hain?*" and the invariable answer would be queries about other people and their fate. "Sometimes we would get annoyed and say, enough, tell us how *you* are, what's happening with *you!* But that is in his character," she shrugs resignedly.

I ask her if she thinks the price Binayak Sen paid for speaking out was disproportionately high. Her answer is immediate and passionate."It was against his grain to be aggressive but it was also against his grain to tolerate injustice, so he had to speak up and in his own way, he spoke up. Being such a compassionate and soft-hearted person, he could not close his eyes to it. He did exactly what a person with a conscience would do, what a civil liberties activist would do.

"As for the price that has been paid or will continue to be paid, it is nothing compared to the price the people there (in Bastar) are paying. So many people are in jail with no legal counsel, no hope, there are so many cases, Naxal cases, people becoming Naxals out of desperation, some are summarily executed as in the case of Kokawada where seven innocent adivasis were killed...when you see all that...

There's that poem by Sarveshwar Dayal Saxena,

Yadi tumhare ghar ke ek kamre mein aag lagi ho, toh kya tum doosre kamre mein soh sakte ho?

Yadi tumhare ghar ke ek kamre mein laashein sadd rahi hon, toh kya tum doosre kamre mein prarthna kar sakte ho?

Yadi haan toh, toh mujhe tumse kuch nahin kehna hai...'

(In your home, if there is a fire burning in one room, can you sleep in the room adjacent to it?

In your home, if there are corpses rotting in one room, can you offer prayers in an adjacent room?

If you can do this, I have nothing to say to you...)

"*Binayak toh nahin kar sakte the* (Binayak could not have done it)" she ends firmly.

By now the cold drink has turned tepid, Anusuya has long since abandoned her scrutiny of me and returned to her books, and

I have a first-hand perspective on Binayak's thinking. But Sudha has a lot more to say. About Binayak's trial, about the case against him, about the massive displacement that is taking place in the parts of Chhattisgarh where she works, amongst the tribals she represents in court and interacts with in their homes. But that's a different story for a different day.

I store it all away as I climb down the stairs of her home, thinking how similar paths, similar choices can so often lead to similar fates and I wonder if some day I will read in the newspapers that Sudha Bhardwaj is in jail for following her conscience.

I wonder too at the magnetic pull, the attraction, the focal point that compelled such immensely talented professionals to gather together in a little-known, dusty small town called Dalli Rajhara.

~

The distance from Raipur to Dalli Rajhara is 124 kilometres in terms of actual mileage. But in terms of a place where history has been created, a workers' movement launched, a collective victory achieved–the distance between the two places is unimaginably vast.

Not many places can claim a past like Dalli Rajhara can. Or be an integral part of so many people's memories, of a period they all claim was "magical".

Dalli Rajhara is a place that is definitely not listed on any tourist itinerary. You pass Bhilai and Durg on the way, with the imposing steel dome-like structures of the Bhilai Steel Plant or BSP catching your attention, then the smaller town Rajnandgaon where I stop for a tea break. The landscape is beautiful here, lush greenery all around, a setting sun. It all appears idyllic till I spot a police station with electric fencing all around. "That's to keep out the Naxalites. If they try to steal arms from the police station, the electric wires will jolt them," says my driver nonchalantly.

By the time I arrive at my destination the evening lamps have been switched on. The single main street is flanked by small shops of all kinds on both sides, casting a yellowish hue all around. At 9 pm it is hardly surprising that there aren't that many people out on the street which is like any other street in small town India.

Grocery shops, small dhabas serving oily food, ubiquitous yellow telephone booths, broken-down lodges where a room costs Rs 145 and the toilet is down the corridor, cycle and motor spare-parts shops owned by sardarjis (even in Dalli Rajhara!), the odd chemist or doctor's clinic with a few straggling people waiting their turn.

Watched by curious onlookers I take a walk down that street, trying to imagine the place twenty-six years ago, trying to imagine how similar or different it might have been. Barring a few new entrants such as telecommunications and those telephone booths, I doubt that Dalli Rajhara has really changed all that much.

Halfway down the street, I halt at a *chowk* composed of a circular, cement structure in the middle of the road. The words engraved on it (and just about readable) are "Shaheed Shankar Guha Niyogi Chowk". I look upwards expecting to see a bust but there is nothing.

I resolve to come back and see it in daylight the next day and make my way to the more tangible monument to Shankar Guha Niyogi—the Shaheed Hospital. As the car winds its way up a slight slope, I can barely make out the shape of an enormous hill on the left of the narrow side lane, stray lights shining like beacons from different corners, lighting it up now and then. On the right of the hill, perched quite high, is a nondescript double-storeyed building, the name "Shaheed Hospital" again barely visible.

It is 10.30 at night but it could as well be 10.30 in the morning, what with the number of patients waiting outside, inside, around the hospital. An ambulance and a jeep parked in front of the narrow entrance are being used to rest against by tired people. For others, they are just obstacles in their path.

As soon as I enter the foyer of the hospital and my eyes adjust to the less-than-bright lights I notice a photograph prominently displayed on a wall. It is a smiling Shankar Guha Niyogi, casting a benign glance at the patients and their relatives and the health workers milling around.

I walk past patients lying on the floor, their arms attached to intravenous drips. Some stare at me with curiosity, others look away vacantly, immersed in their private world of pain and misery. Each patient is also tagged with a cardboard folder exactly like the ones that children use for exams, with the patient's medical details clipped together for ready reference.

I am searching for Dr Saibal Jana, one of the founders of this hospital and a close friend and associate of Binayak Sen. His room is on the ground floor, small, spartan, with an ordinary chair, a desk and an examining table with the usual medical instruments. A calendar is the only other item I can make out in the quick survey I take of the room which is empty of its owner. I wonder how he could spend long hours in this incredibly uncomfortable room.

A voluntary health worker, Soumya Sengupta (a mine worker during the day) starts me on a tour of the hospital, ward by ward, while the search for Dr Jana is on. First, the general ward, Rs 5 per bed, Rs 5 too for all patients allotted a space on the floor, Rs 25 for a semi-private twin-sharing room, Rs 50-100 for a private room. Nobody is using the private room and there are as many patients on the floor as there are in the general wards. I am told that the medicines given are either at very subsidized cost or free for the very poor. Food is not provided by the hospital though care-givers are allowed to cook on the premises.

I walk past crying babies in the maternity ward. The mattresses on the beds have no sheets or pillows, mosquitoes and flies flit in and out, the odour of unwashed bodies fills the air as I walk past patient after patient, relative after relative, sitting or lying down in silence, accepting their condition and their medicine stoically, not knowing or even questioning when or whether they will get better or well...not while I was there at least.

After peering into the operation theatre, the labour room, the x-ray and sonography department, I venture tiredly on to the next floor. Around 11 pm, I catch a glimpse of Dr Saibal Jana. He does not look in the least bit tired, has probably put in more than fourteen hours already since he begins operating at 6.30 am, and is still not ready to call it a day. This, after all, is a hospital that caters to at least 250 OPD (out-patient department) patients and admits fifty patients every day.

Slightly-built, fifty-five years old, not very tall, salt and pepper hair clipped short, a similarly clipped moustache, old-fashioned spectacles, a white lab-coat worn over kurta-pyjama, soft-spoken with a strong Oriya accent, a disarming smile, and comfortable rubber chappals on his feet!

He calmly attends to his last patient after which he greets me and we walk back together towards his charming, thatched-roof, small home adjacent to the hospital. Clicking open the small gate, he ushers me inside. The drawing room has old-fashioned sofas, two steel folding chairs, a center table piled high with old newspapers and an enormous fat lizard near a lamp that crawls out lazily at the sight of us!

Dr Jana's wife Alpana, long-used to his work schedule, serves up a tasty meal. I decide to interview Saibal Jana the next morning but in the meantime she provides me with what turns out to be not just a teaser of what I will hear the following day from her husband and others, but a remarkable account that gives me an insight into their lives in those times.

Alpana Jana is probably not even fifty, petite, dressed in a kaftan. Her large eyes that otherwise look bored and listless, sparkle as she describes the good old days with nostalgia and affection. She grumbles too, but in a good-natured way. "In those times, we used to get Rs 500 as salary, imagine, what can you buy with Rs 500? Pranhita was a baby then, while Ilina sometimes sold saris as well. The workers (belonging to the Chhattisgarh Mines Shramik Sangh, the parent body trade union of the CMM) used to collect funds and give us the same old black urad dal, we could never afford vegetables. So we would add onions and chillies to it to make it taste different!"

She also conjures up an entire day's schedule, the lifestyle of an era, with a few, quick reminiscences. "In those days Dr Sen's outdoor visits would go on and on. Others would finish but not him. He would go on examining patients past 2 pm. All the doctors, their wives, their children, the workers, would be patiently waiting for him. Pranhita would be playing in the adjacent room. Then he would suddenly remember he had forgotten to instruct some patient about something and off he would go on his cycle, all the way back to the patient's home to tell him what to do. And in the meantime, needless to add, the rest would be grumbling with stomachs that were rumbling! He was a perfectionist...he also followed the dictum that you should never do anyone any harm, if you cannot do any good."

As she details the daily rituals and highlights of their shared lives, the picture she is painting for me comes alive in my mind's eye...A little extra money, a treat in store, some fish, bought and prepared by Alpana for the evening meal but alas, in the course of the heated and involved group discussions that are the daily routine, Binayak has polished off the entire lot of fish. And here Alpana was thinking she would make it last a little bit longer... "Then he would admonish me," she says, 'why did you put the fish in front of me? I never even saw it, I ate it while talking.' These were the small, small things that brought flavour into our lives," says Alpana wistfully.

Her voice takes on a different timbre, more serious now as she describes the grand plans that would be made about the work to be done, the enthusiasm amongst all of them at that time, the fact that they never ever thought times were difficult because there wasn't enough money. Or enough clothes or even an almirah, or that they lived in one room...nobody ever felt any sense of deprivation, so deeply connected to their work were they, the union work given to them by Niyogiji. They would work night and day, never felt any loss of energy, never ever said let's do it tomorrow, we are tired today, they never felt like that...if the work had to be done, it was done.

Apart from work, heated political, social, other discussions sometimes continued till 4 am. "Today when I recall those days," Alpana continues, "I feel unless you're inspired you cannot work like that...and we had Niyogiji with us. And our own determination and a vision to reach where we have." Her words are spoken with such passion, they evoke the desire to learn more about the revolutionary atmosphere of that era.

Courtesy Saibal Jana's prior efforts on my account, I am able to track down elusive, forgotten trails of the past, enough people to fill in the spaces so that the picture being painted becomes clearer with every memory stroke added to it.

~

The next morning as I have a piping hot breakfast of *aloo-puri* with Saibal and Alpana at their home, the good doctor is interrupted by different people, each bearing their own chits of personal medical history, all of whom he patiently answers. Then he has to rush off to see a patient urgently, promises to return after attending morning rounds at the hospital to grant me his main interview although Alpana warns me that once at the hospital, he quite often forgets to even have lunch! The proximity to the hospital comes with its own advantages and disadvantages. Sometimes, at night, the cries of patients in pain keep her awake, Alpana says with an involuntary shiver.

Waiting Godot-like for Dr Jana, in the interim, another important *saathi* of those days takes up the tale. Janak Lal Thakur is dressed like the politician he once was, spotless white kurta-pyjama with a striped shawl draped around his shoulders, white hair framing a craggy, 55-odd year old face. A two-time MLA from Dalli Rajhara, Thakur was once an ordinary labourer who used to load material onto trucks. He explains to me the importance of a workers' movement in Dalli, describing the pitiable plight of the 12,000-odd mine workers in the area, extracting ore for the Bhilai Steel Plant in the late Seventies: insufficient rations, fourteen to sixteen hour workdays, low wages, no housing, no electricity, no medical facilities, no education for their children, no trade union support from established unions like INTUC (Indian National Trade Union Congress) and AITUC (All India Trade Union Congress).

Enter the charismatic chemical engineer Shankar Guha Niyogi who had worked earlier at the Bhilai Steel Plant and who fired up the mine workers with his ideas. He told them that they could achieve anything they wanted, for themselves, for society, for the nation, if only they worked for it unitedly. And it didn't matter if they were illiterate or had no technical or legal knowledge; if he set his mind to it, a worker could do anything and everything!

Thus the workers formed their own union, the Chhattisgarh Mines Shramik Sangh (CMSS), to defend their right to a livelihood, for better wages, for basic amenities, for health and education facilities and they fought a long, hard battle, Thakur says with pride. Farmers were also part of this revolution, as Niyogi planned it, with a grand total of seventeen departments, with people allotted different tasks—savings, education, gender issues, prohibition of alcohol, even a provision for sports. And, of course, a department for health.

Enter Dr Binayak Sen. He, along with Ilina, had actually been part of a People's Union for Civil Liberties (PUCL) team investigating the illegal arrest of Niyogi in 1981 under the National Security Act. During his visit to Dalli Rajhara, Binayak interacted with workers and observed that they were looking for someone to lead the health movement and develop a health programme for them in Dalli Rajhara. It seemed providential on both sides. Binayak saw it as an interesting opportunity and Niyogi needed someone like him. Thus a partnership began, with Dr Kundu being part of the original, founding medical team. Dr Saibal Jana joined them a little later.

In those days, government hospitals and even the Bhilai Steel Plant (BSP) hospitals catered mainly to the upper echelons or BSP's regularized workers, certainly not to the contract labourers who worked in the mines or the other less advantaged population of Dalli. It was after a few unfortunate incidents, particularly the death of a pregnant fellow worker, Kusum Bai, who was refused admission at the BSP hospital for her delivery, that the agitated workers decided to build a hospital of their own.

Niyogi consulted with Binayak Sen and the other doctors on this and while the workers literally built Shaheed Hospital, brick by brick, donating money they could probably ill-afford from their meager salaries, Binayak began the medical work from a small garage, using it as a delivery room as well. "Such a big doctor yet one who works with poor people, workers, peasants, tribals, speaks their language, lives with them and lives on in their minds…that is Binayak," says Thakur.

He and Alpana reminisce for a while about the rudimentary beginnings in the garage that the workers emptied out to make room for the clinic after which Alpana calls for Sujata Sukhdevi, an "old-timer" to join us from the hospital.

A portly woman in her late fifties, Sujata is a ward sister and she takes a short break from her hospital duties to take the story forward. She has been part of that story, in those early struggling years, not as a nurse but as a sweeper and she attributes her journey from sweeper to ward sister entirely to Binayak Sen. He is God in her eyes since he placed her on the ladder to progress, taught her skills, taught her independence. He even saw her safely home every day on his cycle, since her husband did not approve of her working in a clinic.

In summer when it got too hot in the garage, Sujata tells us, Binayak would tend to his patients outside, in the shade. As information about him grew, so did the number of patients, from 30-40 in a day to many more, with Dr Kundu and Dr Jana working alongside. If a patient could not afford the fees, he would be treated free of cost. Medicines were also given out, deliveries done, home visits undertaken in which family members were patiently instructed on various aspects of a disease and its cure.

Binayak Sen had a bedside manner quite his own, treating everyone the same, rich or poor. In fact, he had a special affinity towards the underprivileged, he never shied away from poor or unclean patients. He would sit their children in his lap affectionately while tutoring parents and other family members, endearing him to all.

The flashback is not quite over but Sujata's break is, so she leaves even as another "old-timer" takes her place and carries on, almost seamlessly.

Fifty-eight-year-old Amar Bai used to be a mine worker who crushed stone daily for a minimum eight hours on the great big hill that faces the hospital building. Even before the building came up, Amar Bai took turns with five or six other women workers to do voluntary health work taught to them by the doctors. It was part of the 17-point Niyogi plan, of which health was a major component.

"Bhaiyya" or Niyogi and "Sen Sir" or Doc Saab were people who were looked up to, whose ideas were adhered to, whose wishes were respected (This feeling holds good in Dalli Rajhara even today).

Amar Bai explains the routine, "Either Durga, Badan Bai, or I, or others, we would decide among ourselves and volunteer two hours daily after we came back from the mountain." Her tone is matter-of-fact, accustomed as she and her fellow volunteers must have been to a hard life of physical labour. Since the clinic was so small, there was no place to keep patients overnight so they were asked to go home, even after delivery. This went on for a while and then once the decision was taken to construct their own hospital, the workers donated a month's salary and their time and went ahead and built it. And patients finally had a place to stay.

She recaptures the atmosphere of those days when she and her fellow workers shared common dreams. "That was a time of tremendous enthusiasm amongst the public, just imagine 10-12,000 workers, with one goal, poor workers and farmers joining forces, to get adequate work, the right wages for the work, both for workers as well as for peasants...that was Bhaiyya's dream," she says.

Moving on to Binayak, she talks about his unstinting care for patients, his humaneness, his sharing of knowledge freely. A person who was like family for her. Both Binayak and Ilina never categorized people into poor, lower class, tribals, adivasis. For them, people were just people, to live with in harmony. She proudly shares a personal anecdote about how Ilina brought her home-cooked food—fish and eggs, she specifies—when she was unwell and hospitalized, wanting me to know how much she was valued by the Sens. Another intimate and cherished memory is Binayak counselling her on adoption as an option to her being childless, reassuring her that to take care of someone else's child was an even greater blessing. Today Amar Bai's adopted daughter Santoshi is completing her final year B.A. studies and Amar Bai couldn't be happier!

It is stories like these that help me form an idea of the extent of Binayak's involvement with the entire community in Dalli Rajhara in those times, and not just with his patients or friends or fellow doctors. There are plenty of those too, grateful patients like Bimla Bai who still remember how he saved her son by curing his tuberculosis in time, apart from old friends who talk of him with fond nostalgia, vocal on his behalf even if they haven't met him for over a decade.

~

It is lunch time now and predictably Dr Saibal Jana is nowhere to be seen. Alpana suggests I go ahead and meet the other people on my Dalli list and so I head out again, this time to meet C Venkatratnam, a seventy-four-year-old neighbour who says he was friends with both the Dr Sens—Binayak and his father.

I collect his bundle of memories too and they are sharp ones, surprisingly undimmed by age. The sprightly, white-haired neighbour who lived near Binayak in the BSP township locality in Dalli used to be a regular visitor at the Sen home, invited by Deva Prasad Sen, Binayak's father, an army doctor. Venkatratnam grew fond of Bengali food and Binayak of Venkatratnam's rendering of Jaidev's "Geet Govindam."

The old man takes his time telling the story. His captive audience includes his four daughters-in-law (the sons were probably at work), his wife, and Shaheed Hospital health worker Soumya who has accompanied me. "One morning," he begins, "I was singing "Geet Govindam" outside my house. I did not see Binayak but he was behind me, listening intently. He liked my singing a lot and we became friends and they would visit us."

As a doctor, Binayak went on to treat his four sons many times, sometimes at odd hours, even 1.30 am, says Venkatratnam admiringly, adding that Binayak is a very gentle person while wife Ilina is the "dashing" one who fights for good and tolerates no nonsense. He also marvels at the system of fair play practised by husband-wife when it came to household work. "They used to divide the work. If one cooked rice, the other made the rotis; there was total equality."

After showering me with food, hospitality, more personal recollections and numerous messages of goodwill for Binayak and Ilina, the entire family sees me off. It is this abundance of emotion seen in different faces, felt in different homes, echoing in the corridors of the hospital he walked through a million times, through the countless voices of the "old-timers" who worship him, that perhaps helps define Binayak Sen, the man behind the doctor. Someone who is remembered with real affection despite the lack of contact for over a decade, someone who is held up as an example to a younger generation that has only heard stories, someone who is missed sorely and wished back in Dalli Rajhara.

And no one wishes this more than Dr Saibal Jana.

~

Sitting on floor mats with *thaalis* in front of us, eating a very late lunch, Dr Jana and I chat amiably about all the people I have met in my Binayak story-hunt. He adds to the stories, chuckling at one or two funny anecdotes till I beg him to wait for the recording to begin.

Saibal Jana has an interesting way of narrating a tale, it's in the present tense, the sentences are short, and his face is extremely mobile, serious one minute, laughing the next. Binayak is everywhere, he says. "He is in Ganyari, in Shaheed Hospital also. He has not been here permanently since 1987 but after that also, we always feel he is with us. Sometimes we call him, sometimes he comes here too."

In fact, Binayak had begun visiting Shaheed Hospital again, once or twice a week, right upto the winter of 2006 and beginning of 2007, a short while before he got arrested. He used to come on a motorbike, says Dr Jana nonchalantly, as I struggle with the image of the sedate Binayak Sen undertaking a three and a half hour journey on a bike. (Later Binayak tells me he switched to a car because of health issues. Also, that unfortunately he wasn't able to make regular visits due to the distance involved.)

Saibal Jana misses his friend Binayak. Misses his vision, his emotion, the camaraderie of the old days. As a fellow member of the Medico Friends Circle or MFC, Saibal knew Binayak for a very long time but after Binayak's visit to Dalli Rajhara in 1981 as part of the PUCL team investigating Niyogi's arrest, the bond grew stronger. Initially, says Saibal, Binayak thought he would spend just a year in Dalli, so he said he would stay with the workers in Pandagalli, two and a half kilometres from the hospital. He stayed at the home of an iron-ore worker, Bishori Ram, cycling to work daily. People would hail him as the cycle doctor. "He had no beard those days," laughs Saibal. Binayak would spend the entire day with patients and return to Bishori's house at night. Lunch and dinner was provided by the union for everyone, doctors and workers alike. In 1983, when the hospital building was complete and work began in full earnest, Binayak decided to stay longer.

He wasn't involved only in health issues but the lives of people, the troubles they faced. He was very vocal about their struggles, so it was a sort of combination, he was a human being first, then a health worker, then a political worker, who chose to stay on longer. Thus began a friendship and partnership between pioneers and co-founders of a project that was the dream of Dalli's very own hero, Shankar Guha Niyogi. The dream was shared by the 12,000-odd workers and farmers, *Laal-hara* being the official slogan. Central to the vision provided by Niyogi was the Shaheed Hospital—a hospital of the workers, run by the workers, for the workers. The doctors set it up from scratch, creating a system of health care that ought to be replicated a thousand times over in rural India, such is its efficacy, its success, and its affordability. The time spent in setting up the system was a mere four and a half years. Then Binayak went away to continue a similar, but additionally dangerous task in other areas in Chhattisgarh while Saibal stayed back another twenty-two years, consolidating the foundation, never forgetting how and with whose support that foundation was laid.

Today Saibal Jana is the principal guiding force behind Shaheed Hospital. Younger doctors, or a materialistic younger generation, may or may not see him as someone to be admired and emulated, a role model. He has only a MBBS degree from the National Medical College, Kolkata, no post-graduate degree, no other fancy title. Not everyone knows that in his student days he worked with jute mill workers, slum dwellers, organized camps in villages, was part of medical teams that worked in flood-affected areas in West Bengal, Orissa, Andhra Pradesh. No one will give him a medal for the work he does 24×7, 365 days a year. Not that he is looking for medals or even recognition of any kind. He takes his work and its load in his stride, merely smiling when I marvel at the non-stop flow of people demanding his attention. His reminiscences of the early days with Binayak are in fact an unusual break in his otherwise full and hectic schedule, despite the hospital today boasting of eight full-time doctors on its staff.

We learnt a lot of things from Binayak as a doctor, says Saibal frankly. "He's a very sensible person, with a good background, DCH, MD, a brilliant scholar, and he's not a hypocritical doctor. He used to keep books to refer to on the table. If he's seeing a patient and is confused, he will tell the patient, just wait, I will read the book. Sometimes he will make a mistake, when he makes a mistake, he will go to his house and sit there for some time."

In the early eighties, and in a small place like Dalli Rajhara, there was a lot of resistance to new concepts in health care. Indiscriminate and frequent use of injections was the norm rather than the exception and it was an uphill task to re-orient the workers' thinking on this and other related medical issues. Saibal says it was a time when workers were actually very against doctors, so every Friday, Binayak and Saibal would conduct meetings in their office where the workers would start off by asking the doctors why they were anti-injections and the doctors would give detailed explanations. It took quite a while but ultimately people came around. Each evening would be devoted to visits to the workers' *mohallas* where the doctors, having completed their clinic work and home visits through the day, would hold forth on health awareness and even on prohibition, which was one of the main agendas of the CMM.

Binayak was one of the leaders in this campaign, making creative posters, initiating programmes of health education among the workers, arranging exhibitions, forming a health committee of 109 members comprising both male and female mine workers. Amar Bai is one of those initiators of the health education programm, or what Saibal calls peer educators, people who were interested in health work and continue to do so even today without receiving any money or benefits. Health workers would also perform plays that centred round medical issues like AIDS awareness or social issues. The workers' communication skills would improve tremendously after these dramatic experiments.

Meanwhile the doctors continued to face challenges in the field of medicine. Introducing oral rehydration to combat diarrhoea was a major battle those days. The simple and expedient measure of rice water was simply not accepted by the local people. They were extremely suspicious. The doctors would lay out bowls and spoons and ask the mothers to feed their babies with the rice water. On their return to the room, they would find everything intact, the bowls, the spoons, but mothers and babies both would be gone!

Saibal Jana chuckles at the memory of those trying times, adding that Binayak would then track down the patients' addresses from the prescription records and set off with the entire paraphernalia of bowls, spoons, bottles to their homes, sometimes even staying the night, advising people that this was the ideal mode of treatment for diarrhoea. How many doctors would do this? asks Saibal, terming Binayak a "humanist" doctor, one who served patients in a very humane manner, who saw the reasons behind the disease, who was very involved in the workers' plight, in their struggle against the management.

Saibal calls Binayak a political person as well (as indeed were they all) on account of his regular help and attendance at the union office, his participation and advice in the workers' problems and issues with the management, his helping in the preparation of documents that needed to be written in English.

Milestones are mentioned, such as the Rajnandgaon movement in 1984, where striking workers of the 100 year-old cotton mill finally got their due. Even today there are people in Rajnandgaon (60 km away from Dalli), who have not forgotten Binayak's role in the strike...as a doctor, as a helper, as a fellow human being. Another battle was won for the Danitola mine workers from the Danitola quartz mines of the Bhilai Steel Plant in 1986-87. They used to receive only Rs 9 as daily wages as against Rs 50 per day for the Bhilai Steel Plant workers in Dalli Rajhara. Binayak questioned this discrimination, helped draft a resolution and ultimately the Danitola mine workers got parity in wages.

Closer home, at Shaheed Hospital, Binayak introduced the concept of nutrition for paediatric patients, providing *khichdi* for children. The Right to Food stipulated in the Alma Ata Declaration of Health for All by 2000 came much after Binayak's initiatives in this area, says Saibal, branding Binayak one of the pioneers of public health care, someone who has been doing this work for a very long time, from the time of Jayaprakash Narayan. This parallel reference to the leader of the masses, as JP was known, is unintentional but perhaps reflects Saibal's perspective of Binayak.

I ask for personal stories, personal qualities and shades of Binayak that he can share, and Saibal laughs at me indulgently. There are so many stories and so many facets of such a man, he says. Once you set aside the doctor-cum-humanist-cum-political worker combination, Binayak is actually very quiet in nature, a person who has immense faith in people's movements, in deciding what is to be done as a group. This was a quality he shared with Shankar Guha Niyogi, says Saibal.

Start with the mass, Niyogi would say. It is the collective will of people that can change the world; the individual only plays his role in the collective, which is the most important thing and the only way to solve the problems of the people. This philosophy attracted a lot of followers. And Niyogi never used any political jargon, always retaining the common touch which made him hugely popular with the workers. He was a person to whom anyone could go and unburden themselves of their problems, confident of a solution. All of us spent a lot of time with him, chatting late into the night, recalls Saibal. They were all part of history being created in a small little place called Dalli Rajhara, where one man and one union caught a nation's imagination. A man behind a workers' movement that was moving from strength to strength till September 1991 when a bullet halted its trajectory.

Returning to the subject of Binayak, Saibal's eyes twinkle behind his spectacles as he uses the present tense to narrate the daily routine Binayak and he followed. "Washing utensils is a very important part of Binayak's daily journey. Every morning after getting out of bed, he will go to the kitchen, wash the utensils (laughs uproariously) and then he will ask, 'Saibal, *chai chahiye?*' Then he will prepare the tea. He is not a very good cook but he will cook daily. This was our life…"

The tone is unmistakably wistful as he goes on to tell me more about that life. Neither of them had much money those days and yet, he says, if he ever told Binayak he was hungry, Binayak would somehow manage to bring back something to eat! He also remembers Binayak giving him ten rupees for a much-needed haircut one day. The re-telling of even such a small incident gives him such obvious pleasure that I urge him for more such stories and he readily obliges, unwittingly repeating what his wife Alpana had already told me, about Binayak keeping them all waiting for meals and then turning up, contrite, saying, "Okay, okay, I should bring you people something to eat to make up."

Disagreements in work, in friendships, were also settled in the same affectionate manner. And when Binayak and Ilina decided to move on in 1987, out of Dalli, Saibal Jana wished them well, as he does today, but since Binayak was an integral part of a shared life together in Chhattisgarh, the memories refuse to fade away into oblivion. Instead they are summoned up, full frame and sharp focus, as the media spotlight surrounds his old friend, necessitating genuine support and unity.

Saibal shows not a trace of envy at the enormous publicity and public support his friend has been receiving since his arrest. "People love Binayak, as a person, as a dedicated worker, as a health professional who has been in this field for so long, that is why so many people from all walks of life united to support him," he says proudly. He himself supports Binayak not because he is one of his oldest friends and co-founder of Shaheed Hospital but because he likes Binayak's approach towards people, his humanist approach to health. His ability to admit to having made a mistake, his simplicity—these are qualities that attracted Saibal then and now, and make him stand by Binayak come what may.

For both doctors, what has endured is the bond of affection and mutual respect.

~

When I return to Raipur with my Dalli Rajhara tales, almost wide-eyed with the wonder of a lost era, I am eager to hear Binayak's memories of those years, those companions, those pioneers. And he obliges without a pause.

He terms Saibal Jana a unique doctor, someone who not only works 24×7 but whose range of work is something he has never seen before, something everyone can learn from. He emphasizes the enormous responsibility that Dr Jana single-handedly bears today at Shaheed Hospital, a competent staff notwithstanding.

I ask Binayak of the times when they handled it together, hospital work, union work, his memories of Niyogi, and Binayak's face lights up. Some of his reminiscences are naturally similar to what I have already heard from various people in Dalli but what is clear to me is the importance both he and Ilina give to the Dalli Rajhara period in their lives.

In fact Binayak goes so far as to call it a "very heady feeling", the feeling that one is in an area where the politics of the future is being defined. He is of course referring to Niyogi and the workers' movement that he and Ilina were a part of, the entire ethos of which was extremely interesting and challenging, "a great privilege".

He begins his Dalli story. "Ilina and I went to Dalli Rajhara as part of a PUCL investigation into the illegal arrest of Niyogi under the National Security Act. Once in Dalli, it became clear to me that they were looking for someone to lead a health movement and develop a health program for the workers. This seemed like a very interesting opportunity so we came to Dalli— I came first, then Ilina came."

Did he really stay at a worker's home in the beginning, I ask. "Yes, we lived as part of the organization, sometimes we lived in workers' houses, sometimes we lived in the Trade Union office, there was no separate residence of our own," says Binayak matter-of-factly. Later I manage to trace Bishori Ram's widow, Vidya Bai, and see the place where Binayak lived when he first arrived in Dalli. It is a typical village hut with a covered well in front. It is ten years since her husband died and she remembers little about those days but after some prodding and persuasion, recalls that he would often return late at night and sometimes stay over at the union office. She has no clue whatsoever as to why Binayak chose to stay at her home so many years ago, she merely followed her husband's lead in offering hospitality.

For Binayak the most heartwarming part of the Dalli Rajhara years was the shared life they all led. It wasn't just the fact that they had a common goal, a purpose, it was much more, he says. Nobody was better off or worse off; it was all shared. There was no sense of deprivation. "We didn't go into it with the idea that we would sacrifice ourselves. We were just having a very good time," he says nostalgically.

Characteristically he downplays his contribution to the successes of the political movements of that time, for the Rajnandgaon cotton mill workers, the Danitola mine workers, choosing to narrate an anecdote that illustrates a different facet of those days. "There was a *Kabir Panthi mutth* in Nandia which had a long tradition of co-operative farming in a large piece of land that the *mutth* owned and farmed. That whole system came under attack by some vested interests and we fought a long battle to preserve that and ultimately that struggle failed but we learnt a lot from it, so it's not just the successes, some of the most interesting lessons were learnt from the things that failed! A lot of interesting episodes happened in those times, but to look at it as a series of things I did would be quite wrong, all of us together were involved in something that was much bigger."

It is the same spirit of togetherness advocated by Niyogi, and Binayak admits to being influenced by him, admiring him, being privileged to work with him. Niyogiji was a very charismatic figure, he says, he had a lot of ideas about the way politics should be conducted, he had an analysis of society. By virtue of participating in the movement led by him, Binayak was able to acquire a kind of political orientation hitherto lacking since Ilina and he were, at that time, fundamentally, not very political people. Today, in hindsight, Binayak feels that certain things could have been formulated in a different way but concedes that at the time when Niyogi was leading the movement, it (the movement) had its own imperatives and its leader was also part of a particular political tradition that had its very creative aspects as well as shortcomings.

And that is all that he will say on the issue of differences with Niyogi or certain problems that ultimately led to Binayak and Ilina leaving Dalli towards the end of 1987 to move to a Mission hospital in Tilda, mostly to remain rooted in Chhattisgarh. Instead he mentions the numerous occasions that Niyogi met and talked to them, asking them to return to Dalli. Binayak had made up his mind to do so, had in fact resigned from his job at Tilda but then Niyogi was murdered and that changed the whole scenario. For everyone.

Ilina Sen remembers the last meeting with Niyogi with sadness and regret. "We had gone to meet him about two weeks before he was killed. He kept asking us to stay on for dinner. As we were coming back, we passed a fish seller. Niyogi said, 'Come on, let's buy some fish, change your mind, stay for dinner.' But we had left our children at home so we had to leave. That was the last time we saw him."

Interestingly Ilina Sen echoes many of Alpana's views of the Dalli Rajhara period in their lives, and both of them were not mere supporters of their husbands' work at Shaheed Hospital but active and equal participants in the movement. Women were treated as an integral part of the workers' struggle and not because Niyogi or Binayak Sen decreed it so, but because the women themselves were very much a part of it all. In fact, Ilina credits the women workers of Dalli and that period of her life for providing her with a "whole heritage of strength". It helped her stay strong through the harrowing two-year jail term of her husband much later.

The Dalli Rajhara she describes is very different from the present-day unremarkable, nondescript, almost sleepy town that I have been zigzagging across in my search for people who remember the past. Ilina calls it a place which was very "live", where there was a lot of activity, cultural activity, a lot of music late into the night, a lot of camaraderie. Everybody relating as equals, without barriers of caste or class, different kinds of people coming together—middle class people, workers, intellectuals—it was an experience she terms "fantastic" and something she had never experienced or imagined, having grown up in a middle class environment.

The sharing was the best part, according to Ilina, who made the transition easily, living with and mingling happily with the workers. Not so easy for her mother to accept, though, she tells me wryly, describing a visit where she took her along for a cultural event thinking her mother who shared her love for music and was a singer herself, would enjoy the evening. At the end of the programme, Ilina found her mother weeping. She told Ilina she could not bear the idea of her sitting together with "these" people and singing and this was not why she had sent her to good schools! It took her two years to understand her daughter's chosen way of living.

For Ilina and her daughters however, this was never an issue. Pranhita's upbringing was typical of the kind of lives they led in Dalli in those years. She grew up among many families, calling three different women "Ma". Ilina smiles at the memory. "Today Pranhita calls me Ma but when she was a baby, she had Ashoma (Niyogi's wife Asha), Sheshuma (a lady named Shivbati Sahu who cared for her) and Ilinama. My younger daughter Billo did not have access to that period. The whole concept of individual families that lived in separate houses and shared things in a small unit–that simply did not exist. We lived in a house where seven people lived with us, then some people shifted out to give us some space, but then other people moved in, so yes, we all lived together, ate together, particularly dinner."

Like Binayak, Ilina calls it a "life of privilege", of richness, even though cash was often in short supply. The Dalli experience also taught her to never be afraid of not having enough money! She lost her fear of financial insecurity forever, firmly believing that something will always work out if you are rational and use your options carefully. She tells me how selling her heavy Benarasi silk saris was one such option at a time when there was absolutely no money and the union too had no money, and she thought why not get rid of wedding saris that she was never going to wear? And so she did, today laughing uproariously at her ingenuity so many years ago.

She also corrects an impression that many people mistakenly have and tend to hold on to, that Binayak was the one who went into a difficult arena and his family tried to keep up with him. She *always* kept up her own work, kept one foot in academia as it were, continuing with her PhD, doing her fellowship in addition to all the other work at Dalli. "Binayak and I are different in that sense," she says, "when he opted for Dalli or for human rights work, he gave everything to it. But I have not done it with anybody, not in my relationships, not in my work. I have always kept a balance."

She agrees with her husband that living with Niyogi, whom she describes as a brilliant though also a difficult person in many ways, was like being part of history. So why did they leave? I ask her. Her answer is rather more detailed than Binayak's one-liner about differences of opinion and about ultimately wanting to return to Dalli on Niyogi's request. Simply put, towards the end of their seven-year stay in Dalli, both Binayak and Ilina wanted to widen the scope of their work. Shaheed Hospital was in any case up and running successfully. Binayak was more involved in trade union work than medical work, Pranhita had grown up a little bit, Ilina had completed her PhD and wanted to contribute a lot more in the field of people-centred social research, not really possible in Dalli at that time due to a lack of basic amenities. There was not even a proper telephone facility. In order to talk to one's family, one had to travel to Durg, 83 kilometres away, book a trunk call and wait. So even while wanting to continue, Ilina did not want to close other options and limit their work to only trade union activity.

She is honest enough to admit to a fear that twenty years later she would look back at her work and regret lost opportunities. She wanted to research, to write but it didn't seem possible to do that in Dalli. Niyogi had wanted to set up something in Raipur that combined writing and publishing, she explains, but because of his time constraints and trade union work in Bhilai, this did not materialize.

Binayak and Ilina's decision of setting up a trust of their own (that later took the form of Rupantar) caused some unhappiness and resentment, but she clarifies that these were not major issues and that Niyogi ultimately supported them and Rupantar. The reason that Niyogi is such an integral part of everyone's memories of their lives, their work, their decisions, in Dalli in those years is perhaps hard for an outsider to understand but not so for those who spent invaluable time with him, sought his guidance, believed in his vision. The words "*Bhaiyya ka sapna tha...*" are repeated so often by "old-timers" in Dalli that you come to accept them all as co-owners and participants of that dream.

~

Walking the streets of Dalli Rajhara today, I sense that past carelessly forgotten, indeed almost cast away. Much like the empty Shaheed Shankar Guha Niyogi Chowk. In the harsh daylight glare, the words seem even more faded. I make my way to the bus stand nearby, having been told that it too was named after the slain leader. But the ordinary structure bears no such name and a curious on-looker informs me that it was named Niyogi

Bus Station earlier but not any more. There is only one thing left to do before I leave Dalli. Armed with directions given by Saibal Jana, I set off to meet the Niyogi family to ask them about their ties with Binayak Sen.

The Niyogi home is not very far from Shaheed Hospital. The car does not go all the way since the lane is quite uneven, so I walk through narrow alleys on a cloudy afternoon, asking helpful people peering from windows, watching me navigate puddles on the muddy lane, "*Niyogiji ka ghar kahan hai?*" Following directions, I pass through a small, creaking iron gate and wend my way through a grassy path to knock at the low-slung door of a thatched-roof hut.

The house is small, built of bricks and mud, similar to those adjoining it, with the only difference being my own sense of awe, my feeling of anticipation. A plump young girl with a cherubic face, salwar-kameez clad, opens the door. Her name is Mukti (meaning freedom) and she is the youngest of the Niyogi children, all their names symbolic, the elder sister being Kranti (revolution), the brother being Jeet (victory). She smiles a greeting and calls for her mother to join us.

Asha Niyogi is perhaps in her early to mid-fifties, simply clad in a cotton sari, her face a little on the chubby side, like her daughter's. She is slightly taken aback at my questions, at my unannounced presence, but with true Dalli hospitality and tradition, soon warms up, offering detailed answers and easy friendship.

While the by-now familiar phrases of praise for Binayak ring unmistakably true in her heavily Chhattisgarhi-accented Hindi, the unexpected, occasional use of English words like "conciliation meetings" catch me unawares!

Asha Niyogi's recollections of "the heady days" are especially important because they constitute an "insider" point of view—

many important workers' meetings addressed by her husband took place in their home in her presence. Even more interesting are her own interpretations of why the good old days can never return, why the magic that is lost can never be restored, why she misses more than just her dead husband's physical presence.

For the next two hours as she goes back in time, the longing mixed with regret in her voice is a tangible presence in the tiny room. She sits a little above me on the single large bed dominating the room and I sit on a stool facing her. Mukti watches us silently. A large portrait of a smiling Niyogi adorns the wall behind her. Asha begins by describing the *seva bhavna* with which Binayak came to Dalli, living amongst workers, working for their health, visiting village homes, explaining about illnesses and cures, preventive measures and social issues. "When he first came here he didn't even have a quarter to live in, and before Shaheed was established, he started his work, *woh ghoom ghoom ke ilaj kari*. He himself is such a good doctor and such a good person that many workers learnt from him and became '*acchhe insaan*', (good people)", says Asha admiringly.

I ask her about her husband's influence over Binayak's life and she smiles shyly. "Well, that question only Binayak can answer, what I can tell you is that both Binayak and Ilina wanted to work with *seva bhavna* and that is why they liked my husband since he was always involved in people's work, be it education, awareness, he was forever helping others and very happy doing so. Dr Sen saw this and was inspired to emulate him and till today he is doing it, isn't he? In medicine, in the field of human rights?" She is up to speed with the current events in Binayak's life, keeping track. He is family after all.

Today too, whenever Binayak visits Dalli, even if it is for a very short while, he visits the Niyogis, she informs me proudly, conveying how strong a relationship the two families continue to share. But it is the sharing of the early days that I want to know more about and like Saibal, Alpana, and the Sens, her eyes brighten at the prospect of re-living the past, if only by telling me about it.

Dr Sen, as she refers to Binayak rather formally, would do his "doctor" work but also help her husband with conciliation meetings, other "big" meetings and programmes of the workers. In those days when the union had just been formed, there were numerous problems...no money, no facilities such as phones. If there was any untoward incident, one had to walk or cycle to Naya Bazaar. Overriding all of these difficulties were the primary demands and needs of the workers. For their rights, for daily wages, for medical facilities.

"Often workers would die at the mere thought of going to a hospital for a cure for their illness." What she means really is that hospitalization was an unaffordable option for workers in Dalli at that time. All that changed with Shaheed Hospital and the workers' own efforts, she says with pride.

This same three-room *mitti-ka-bana ghar*, mud house, as she describes it, with a large-ish backyard doubling up as a kitchen garden, was home to the many community discussions and dinners held over those tumultuous years when Niyogi, Binayak, Saibal and others would assemble together and talk late into the night. What did they talk about? I ask her. They talked about union matters, about the nation, about politics, she says unhesitatingly.

Didn't they ever talk about their wives and children? I quiz her laughingly, why was it always the nation and politics? She smiles in answer, not quite understanding my point of view. "They never had the time. They would attend meetings, listen to the workers' demands, take decisions, there was so much to do, often they would return at 2.30 am. *Ek baar gaye kaam pe toh gaye*, once gone they were gone, they would return sometimes even at

3-4 am. By then, naturally the children would be sleeping. Days would go by without their even seeing their father's face!"

I continue to prod her, finding it amazing that there was such willing acceptance of such little family time. Didn't Ilina or she ever complain or ask for more attention? She narrates an incident in reply, chuckling at the memory so many years later. They all had a celebration dinner at Binayak's home when Pranhita was just twenty days old. Soon after, Niyogi had an accident and was laid up in bed in hospital for a while and Binayak had to go for conciliation meetings in his stead, leaving Ilina to cope all day long with an infant all by herself. That caused some tension for a bit, she says laughingly. But no one really complained!

She speaks of the Binayak-Niyogi relationship in glowing terms, remembering their last meeting in Bhilai where Niyogi had urged Binayak to come back and work together again and Binayak had agreed to think about it. After Niyogi's murder, Binayak was very upset recalling that statement, she tells me sadly. Binayak's sense of loss over not just Niyogi's death but over what might have been another beginning for them all, is reflected in Asha's memories too. "I remember Dr Sen often. When he visits us, I feel good, he is our very own person from our old days. But I feel bad remembering those days when we lived together, ate together, worked together. I miss that time so much," she says emotionally.

The union was a family, everyone lived and worked and ate together like a family, work was shared, food was shared, whatever little there was, *daal-bhaat, roti-sabzi*. Everyone felt they were doing good work, no one thought one person was working harder or another person was receiving less, everything was shared. If there was a problem everyone worked towards finding a solution. No worker was discriminated on any basis of caste or status, whether he or she was rich or poor.

"How did it all change? Why did that feeling diminish? Everyone is scattered now, even in the union, I feel awful that *woh baat nahin hai aaj jo un din thi.* The union is there, the work is going on, the hospital is there too but that feeling is not there. Even those people who weren't even a part of those days feel nostalgic about them. They say if Niyogiji were alive today, Dalli would be Dilli (Delhi). He would have led a *sangharsh* (revolution), taken it forward and made it Dilli."

"Dr Sen came here inspired by the union and by my husband and today too there are people here who want to rise up and be counted and show the world what they are capable of but there is no one to show the way," she ends passionately.

~

Her words "Dalli could have been Dilli" continue to ring in my ears, long after I have bade the Niyogi family farewell, leaving the neglected home of a neglected hero, in silent contemplation. Driving out of a historic town that doesn't seem to have much use for that history today, I make a final halt at another historic destination. A small, nondescript, gray house inside the Hudco colony of the Bhilai Steel Plant (BSP) in Bhilai, where a thirty-year-old man, a natural inheritor of a famous legacy he may or may not live up to, waits to share stories of a past he has only heard about and a recent present he claims to have tangentially shared with Binayak Sen.

Jeet Niyogi, a 12th Standard pass-out, has been training for the last one year in the social service out-reach programme for villages within a 16 kilometres radius of the BSP where his father once worked. He is working for income-generation schemes that include the making of *papads*, pickles and *chulhas*. Ironically he has been allotted the same house that his father once lived in, and was murdered in. In fact there is a sign displayed outside that seems to have been put up a long time ago since the board and the words look old and shabby. It reads that this is the home of slain martyr Shaheed Shankar Guha Niyogi and gives the date and time of his death as 3 am, Sept 28, 1991.

Jeet shows me around the house with perfect composure, pointing out the room where his father was killed while he was sleeping, through an open window. The pane is cracked and I do not ask how long it has been so. Some things are better left unsaid. Jeet was fourteen years old when his father was assassinated. He frankly admits that he never really knew his father when he was alive and that he learnt a lot more about him after his death! About his thinking, about his work with the union, about his successes. He was too young then, he says, and didn't know much about all this. As a child, he remembers spending very little time with his father, much less chatting with him.

But he doesn't consider his childhood any different from that of others in Dalli Rajhara. They all grew up in the backdrop of *andolans*, *juloos*, rallies, *bandhs*, strikes on a regular basis—it was part of their working class heritage almost from birth, says Jeet matter-of-factly.

He is equally quick to dismiss financial difficulties faced by the Niyogi family after his father's murder, merely asserting that today things are looking up, as apart from him, both his sisters also work. The elder one, Kranti, teaches in a government school and the younger one Mukti, in a BSP school. "It isn't as if we have become rich today but we are able to manage our household," he smiles.

The smile vanishes when he talks about the greatest difficulty that the family faced and continues to face—the disintegration of the organization built so painstakingly by his father. Jeet has formed a breakaway faction of the CMM called the Jan Mukti Morcha, which is not against the CMM but differs from it even while keeping alive the best traditions laid down by his father.

And it is here that Binayak Sen has re-entered the life of the little boy who barely remembers him in his home town Dalli Rajhara as the doctor who they all went to when they fell ill! As an adult, Jeet Niyogi proudly lays claim to consistent support from Binayak ever since the Jan Mukti Morcha was formed in 2001. "He came for each of our programmes, regularly supported us."

There is no need for me to ask him whether Binayak is a role model for him as the admiration is obvious and overwhelmingly enthusiastic. Jeet accompanied Binayak on several conferences, rallies, and meetings, including one with the Governor of Chhattisgarh. He saw Binayak speak his mind (at a seminar on the Salwa Judum), boldly and with strong conviction, without any fear of the consequences or retaliatory action. "He is a person who just does not care *ki aage peeche koi hai ki nahin! Jo bhi bolte hain damdaari ke saath bolte hain, taakat ke saath. Kabhi peeche mudke nahin dekhte ki police arrest kar sakti hai ya meri baat ka log virodh kar sakte hain. Agar virodh karna hai, toh karna hai, bas!* (He does not care about the consequences of his acts, whether he will get arrested or whether anyone will protest against his words or deeds. If he wishes to oppose something, he will do it!) I truly admire this quality," says Jeet with unbridled ardour.

Later I ask Binayak about Jeet's organization and he confirms providing the young man with encouragement and support. He also completely empathises with Asha Niyogi's disillusionment with the situation in Dalli Rajhara, agreeing that major setbacks have taken place and the promise of those early days has been belied.

The Dalli Rajhara story with all its different players and role models laid the foundation stone for the kind of choices Binayak Sen was to make many, many years later.

Choices that would cost him and his family dear but choices that were inevitable.

Just tracking his seven odd years in Dalli provides enough clues and insights into the definitive orientation Binayak had acquired that later led to his uncompromising, unflinching stance on uncomfortable issues that most people would push under the carpet in a heartbeat.

But Binayak Sen is not "most people" and the Dalli Rajhara story was just the beginning...

Chapter Three

ROOTS

Vellore

Sara Bhattacharji is almost exactly the kind of person you would imagine a close friend of Binayak Sen to be...a highly qualified MD in community medicine from the Christian Medical College (CMC) in Vellore, dedicated doctor of "family medicine", heading a unique low cost hospital amidst the urban slums of Vellore, with a strong outreach and training programme for CMC medical students and interns. Yet another "elite" professional who took the road less travelled and chose to spend thirty years of her life providing quality health treatment to the poor at no or very minimal cost.

The LCECU (Low Cost Effective Care Unit) or Scudders Ward (named after Ida Scudder, the founder of CMC) is part of a nondescript building in the heart of the bustling town, a modest sign proclaiming its equally modest appearance. I ask for directions to her office and climb a ramp to the first floor where she is sitting quietly at her desk, reading.

Prematurely white hair, a remarkably unlined, youthful face for her fifty-eight odd years, a calm and competent demeanour, a confident, frank, very cooperative approach to my questions about Binayak, both the past and present years. She has after all, known him for forty years!

For the next ninety minutes the animated discussion is interrupted only twice by respectful nurses wanting her permission to go off duty and by my request to turn off the noisy whirring fan in the small room. Sara's office is truly basic, a table, two plastic chairs, a window that overlooks the ramp, a cupboard for storage— no frills or furnishings.

Her work speaks louder than her soft voice: nineteen years spent in the department of community health. The twenty-seven-year old Scudders Ward that she heads today, treats around 30,000 out-patients and admits 1000 in-patients per year, conducting 250 surgeries as well as treating chronic illnesses like TB, diabetes, hypertension, apart from infectious diseases. The unit's outreach programme in the slums taps into volunteers and other community based organizations with similar values, to address the needs of the poor and disadvantaged. By any standards, it is an astonishingly impressive body of work. And yet she tells me in the very first few minutes of our conversation that she feels ashamed that she cannot be the kind of person Binayak is and how much she admires him for what he did. "Many of us who work in health do a lot of work in terms of helping those who are sick or marginalized or poor, in terms of giving the treatment but when the water gets hot, then we move back very quickly," says Sara reflectively.

She explains that doctors who work with very poor people realize over time that the issues that keep them poor are far too complex and so it is much easier to treat the fever or cold or cough. The difficulty is magnified when the fever, cold and cough will force you to look at why it is there, why some child is just not getting better or not growing, not putting on weight, is malnourished. If you really search for answers then you get into troubled waters.

Doctors tend to hide behind the technology, the aura of knowledge, the conventional solutions rather than questioning the status quo or making statements about health and human rights, says Sara. Even those who agree may not have the courage to be so vocal. So in some measure the great groundswell of support for Binayak comes from many doctors who felt that he is doing what they should actually be doing. In the end, though, Sara admits that everyone does what they have to do. I admire her honesty and say so.

She smiles and agrees with my observation that her work is very similar to Binayak's. "But I didn't push the human rights angle. When we were in college it wasn't an important issue at all. We were all having fun, we were also fired up with the idea of socialism but when you are students, it's all nebulous, your hands are not in the hot water yet."

Binayak's life, according to Sara, is so much beyond health. All his work, the connections—medical, social, political—have impacted who he is, how he thinks, his very strong passion for human rights which came through in what he was doing. His whole idea of health care at low cost...Shaheed Hospital, training health workers, running clinics, de-professionalization of medicine, breaking down of hierarchy, his ability to share medical knowledge with everybody else...these are important things about Binayak, she tells me.

I ask about the early college years, the memories, the fun moments and she readily obliges, breaking quite a few imagined stereotypes in my mind. "When I joined CMC in 1968," Sara begins, "Binayak was in his second year and their class was in the middle of its first big exam in physiology, biology, anatomy and they were exempt from attending classes so it was only after December that this whole new group of people came into my view. Among them was Binayak...a very fun loving, loud, active, involved kind of a student, although he was also a very serious person. But he had a hearty laugh, he still has it." The young Binayak enthusiastically went onstage, even playing a female role in a play called "The Amorous Prawn", complete with big hips, big breasts, all made up! She tells me that in college Binayak was rather noisy and at the centre of all the fun.

He was a very good student academically, kept up with all his classes, was universally liked by everyone in the class and very involved in all extracurricular activities like college plays which Sara says were very good productions. And then there was the Students Christian Movement (SCM) to which Sara belonged. Binayak, who was not a Christian, used to attend meetings of the SCM and ask outrageous questions, initially shocking Sara but later helping her question her own core beliefs. He would ask questions about man's relationship with God, and personal salvation...Sara describes these as topical issues of the sixties and seventies.

I envy them for the idealistic era they were students in, so different from the materialistic one today where the young aspire to a Ferrari at the age of twenty-six. She agrees. "As teachers today we are really struggling to address these issues with this generation in a language which they will understand. Because in one sense the young one who is aspiring for a Ferrari at twenty-six is in a completely different world from mine. And yet we need to fire this young person with the same vision and dream, so how does one do that? Is it possible to keep the Ferrari and be pro-poor? I don't know. I think there is a trade-off between how much you have and you possess and how much you will be able to do for other people."

According to Sara Bhattacharji, Binayak Sen has internalized, interpreted and fully taken forward the ideals that CMC Vellore has stood for over the last 110 odd years, combining medical care with the other needs of the disadvantaged. A sort of holistic approach to healing.

Binayak wasn't one of those people who had a "conversion" experience at CMC. His basic values, his belief systems, his compassionate nature were very much an integral part of his personality, courtesy his upbringing, the family he belonged to. The college merely honed these qualities. (Binayak himself credits CMC with shaping his path, his decisions, the trajectory of his life.)

Sara's favourite Binayak story is about the time he realized, as a new intern, at the end of a gruelling day, that he had written a prescription for lasix (a diuretic) for a patient without including the required potassium supplement. The patient had gone home by this time. Binayak went to the medical records department and looked up the patient's address, went to the pharmacy where he bought the potassium, then sallied forth, taking various village buses (he, a Bengali struggling without knowing the local languages in rural Tamil Nadu) to the patient's village where he delivered the supplement.

This oversriding concern for the patient's needs in totality, was to later on become the hallmark of Binayak's modus operandi, and stories such as these became legion.

~

Vellore is pretty much CMC-centric. That's really what it is famous for and has been for quite a while, despite newer "attractions" such as the Golden Temple being touted as tourist destinations. While the main hospital is in the heart of town, the college campus is about 7 kilometres away in Bagayam.

Like most elite college campuses, this one too is spread over vast, well-maintained land, almost 200 acres I am told, with beautiful old trees and stately old stone buildings where, to use the old-fashioned description given by the college itself, "young men and women live and study medicine". Situated on the impressive campus are the student hostels, departments of pre-clinical sciences, the homes of many staff members and the Big Bungalow, which was the founder, Dr Ida's residence and now serves as a guest house for visitors, as does the Big Bungalow Annexe. It is here that I am headed to meet Binayak Sen again, this time to rewind and pause...and recapture memories of a different day.

Binayak is in CMC Vellore for an extended stay because Ilina is undergoing medical treatment. He himself had earlier requested the Chhattisgarh state government to allow him to get treatment at his alma mater for his heart-related health problems but was turned down.

After receiving bail, one of his first priorities, after visiting his mother in Kolkata, was a medical check-up, an angiography at CMC, which fortunately showed that his heart condition did not need surgical intervention and could be controlled with medication. But Ilina was diagnosed with breast cancer, a mastectomy was performed successfully and chemotherapy sessions prescribed.

~

Binayak, Ilina, Pranhita and Aparajita (Billo) are staying together in one large room in the Big Bunglow Annexe. Along with a small kitchenette and a bathroom, it seems cool, comfortable and functional but as a home for more than four months?

It is hard to not feel enormous empathy for the difficult times that the Sen family continues to face, hard to intrude on their privacy but Binayak and Ilina both welcome me into their temporary home with smiles and spontaneous hugs. Billo is unwell and Binayak is concerned about her fever not coming down. Ilina reassures him. After a cup of coffee that Binayak makes at Ilina's insistence, we shift to a more formal setting in the building opposite the Annexe for the interview.

I ask him why as a student he chose CMC Vellore and the answer is (absurdly) simple. "My father met a CMC Vellore graduate in the army and asked me to take the exam. I took it, was selected and came to Vellore. I didn't know a great deal about CMC but I had heard about it from other graduates of CMC and once I came here, I liked it very much."

I rewind just a little bit more and want to know at what point he decided he wanted to become a doctor. "Since my father was a doctor, I was interested in the profession of medicine, I used to read novels about it, the kind that many people would have read, A J Cronin etc. but I also read Albert Schweitzer, I read about the history of science, history of medicine at a very early stage. My father encouraged me in all this. He was also a good doctor and the kind of influences he brought to bear…I can give you an example: there is a textbook of medicine I valued greatly which I have unfortunately lost, Saville's "System of Clinical Medicine". My father had written on the flyleaf, 'Bury one another's burden'. So I think that influence came through, that was part of why I wanted to become a doctor," says Binayak.

"I'm told you also sat for the IIT entrance exam. Why would you do that?" I ask curiously.

"Yes, well, it was coming up and so I took it. I passed it also," he says with a slightly self-satisfied air which is very endearing because it is so rare in Binayak.

I am in Vellore to discover for myself the young Binayak of the 1966 batch, what he was like, what the major guiding forces were in his student days, what ideology shaped his thinking, the choices he would make later on in life. As it happens, this picture is drawn more clearly by the people around Binayak rather than Binayak himself. His lasting impressions of the CMC days, other than the "very busy schedule of extracurricular activities, especially theatre," are more a tribute to the quality of the teaching of medicine, which he terms as very good, and of the teachers. He talks of the chance to interact very closely with members of the faculty, to take part in discussions, to visit them in their homes, sit and listen to music with their teachers, have the opportunity to become close to them, as rare privileges for a medical student. He doesn't know many medical colleges that allow that kind of thing any more or even at that time.

The other significant part of his student life he remembers vividly are the institutionalized discussions courtesy the Students Christian Movement. "We had ideological discussions from a Christian point of view and even though I was not a Christian, I was an associate member, no one ever excluded me. It was a forum where we could discuss many of the fundamental issues," he reminisces.

Research was another unique feature at CMC, he says. The pride is low-key but very much evident in his praise of his college. "We were given the scope to exercise our freedom of enquiry. Many of my colleagues were able to go much further than me and actually participate in research projects while they were still students. There are students who have done first-rate research in this way. In other medical colleges this is an extremely rare phenomenon, here it is common."

The best part by far, illustrated also by the rock-solid support that the CMC fraternity as a whole provided to Binayak later in his hour of need, is what he calls the bonding. "Since the student body was so small—sixty students in a class—there was a lot of intimacy. That bonding has stayed. It's now forty years since I left CMC, and there are people with whom I may not have corresponded in forty years but when I do, it feels like I am a member of that immediate circle," he says emotionally.

On a lighter note, I ask him about his favourite haunts so I can go check them out the very next day. He laughs and mentions just one. "Just here, near the front gate, there's a corner shop, it was just a thatched roof hut, we used to spend a lot of time there, now I believe it's become a bit more sophisticated."

A few hours later, as I leave the college campus and walk to the main gate with Ilina, she points out the corner shop to me. She remembers it too, of course.

Her own memories of CMC are happy ones too, and she shares them with me sitting in the same library. "I came here as a bride, just after we got married. I must have been twenty years old. It was the first place I moved to. When you actually start living together you start getting to know the person, getting to know the place," Ilina says smilingly. (Binayak and Ilina were married in Kolkata in 1973 and came to Vellore for Binayak to complete his post-graduation in paediatrics.)

Ilina was just out of Kolkata's Lady Brabourne College when she took up a job teaching at a school set up by the CMC staff for their children. Even though at that time she had no formal education in teaching (she completed her PhD on the declining sex ratio in India later), she thoroughly enjoyed her experience, interacting with students of the 11th Standard, reaching out to them, understanding them. Of course things were difficult too, she says, she didn't know any Tamil then and doesn't know much even today but making all the adjustments was an adventure and she enjoyed it hugely!

Walking through the leafy lanes intersecting the various buildings of the sprawling campus, it is not hard to imagine a khadi-clad

Binayak (that is what he wore most of the time, even then, according to one of his professors!) treading the same path more than forty years ago. College campuses have a way of freezing time, the routine rarely changes, over weeks, years, decades. Neither does the animated discussion over *chai* at the corner shop, or classical plays or concerts performed with enthusiastic zeal.

What *was* unique in Binayak's time was the environment and the kind of people his class interacted with as part of their daily student routine. People who worked at CMC for ideological, not just professional reasons, who believed and reinforced the basic ethos of the college: Dr Paul Brandt who explored the problem of leprosy, Dr Mary Verghese, founder of the institute for the physically handicapped and herself a paraplegic, both a visible presence, a part of the milieu in which Binayak studied. Departments that were concerned with the social dimension of medical issues...all of this happening in the late sixties and early seventies which saw the flowering of so many new ideas and influences...the entire sixties ethos with its social revolution or counterculture movement, the anti-war wave, the rise of feminism and the new Left, the music of Bob Dylan, Joan Baez, the Rolling Stones, Janice Joplin, Jimi Hendrix, the Beatles...

How could Binayak *not* have been touched by the atmosphere around him?

~

His teachers, whom I track down quite easily, (at least the ones that still live in Vellore) share their recollections of their student as well as the institution that contributed towards shaping the direction he would choose to take later on, in his life and career.

Offering warm hospitality and old-world courtesy in their well-maintained, comfortable bungalows where they have chosen to retire, Dr P Zachariah, former head of the Physiology Department of CMC and Dr Jacob John of the Paediatrics Department where Binayak did his post-graduation, speak of past triumphs and future expectations from their stellar student. Even after a gap of forty years, Dr Zachariah remembers not just Binayak's academic brilliance but his Leftist, socialist attitude that led him to critique, question things, to be an intellectual rebel of sorts.

Binayak's decision to take up paediatrics led to his interaction with extremely good scientists involved with malnutrition, says Professor Zachariah. His MD thesis was to be an eye-opener on poverty and the impact it had on the child population. Binayak took not just a scientific approach to malnutrition but a holistic one. He visited the families of malnourished children and quickly understood that this is not a clinical phenomenon but a socio-economic issue. Gradually his entire attitude towards medicine changed.

Dr Jacob John remembers his student as a little bit of an odd person but very gentle, very kind, always unruffled, quiet in an efficient way. Wearing *khadi* almost always, and known as a Gandhian. I find it a bit strange to hear Binayak remembered as a Leftist intellectual rebel *and* a gentle Gandhian in a space of three hours by his teachers.

Dr Zachariah continued to interact with Binayak, even after the CMC student days were over. He remembers being enormously impressed by his work with displaced people in a clinic Binayak was running in a humble place which didn't even have a roof, just three walls! But within CMC, for so many years, not much was known about him because he wasn't someone who would work within the alumni circle, he was always a loner. I question him about the 'loner' aspect, pointing out that Binayak admits to drawing strength from the collective, from working together. Dr Zachariah clarifies: "Even in a group he is a loner. These ideological-oriented people, they walk the same route, but they often walk by themselves, so even this group is an ideological linkage rather than one of a personal relationship."

People who have strong commitments, people who swim against the current, are also quite angular, he feels. They have rough edges, sharp corners because they are so devoted to what they believe in. At a personal level they are difficult to get along with because they are single-minded in their commitment to whatever they have undertaken. I ask him if Binayak is really 'angular'. No he is not, is the answer. Binayak is soft spoken, says Dr Zachariah, but he will stick to his guns, he will not make a noise about it, he is not angular in his interpersonal relations but he is very much his own man. That is true of all such people who go in for something like this, they believe in it and that is what gives them fulfilment. Otherwise you cannot sustain it. Living a life like that is really because you *want* to do it.

"We have the Paul Harrison award at CMC and the fact that each year someone gets it means that at least one person in CMC is doing something like this," he says with pride. Binayak Sen received the Paul Harrison award from his alma mater in 2004 "in recognition of his outstanding contribution to society". The citation reads: "Dr Binayak Sen has been true to the spirit and vision of his alma mater...He has broken the mould, redefined the possible role of the doctor in a broken and unjust society, holding the cause much more precious than personal safety. CMC is proud to be associated with Binayak and Ilina Sen. He is a role model for the students and staff of CMC..."

Dr Jacob John talks about the award: "Very prophetically the Paul Harrison citation says this man is putting his reputation at stake for a cause...and it turned out to be true. He is a good and great man and we all admire him for that."

I ask the obvious question: Is Binayak a role model for CMC students today? His answer is frank. "Our aim is to train students to come out in a mould of not the worldly doctor but in a social consciousness role. We can't guarantee what the response will be..."

I ask Sara the same question and she shakes her head in reply. "Certainly I have heard students say that in this day and age when our role models are cardio-thoracic surgeons who make Rs 1 lakh a day, we lack a role model like Binayak." Later on another friend of Binayak's, a fellow MFC (Medico Friends Circle) member, Manisha Gupte, sums it up succinctly and honestly. "In a society that we dream of, Binayak will be a role model but right now he is not...he may be great to put up as a photograph in your living room, at a distance...my neighbour's son can be like him, but not mine!"

The challenge lies in enabling young doctors to see the stark reality and not run away from it, to remain engaged with it, otherwise, according to Sara, these are marginal areas of medicine where you find very few people. And sometimes many of the young groups that go in with vision and understanding, face burn-out very quickly if they cannot find others to join them, replace them, and then they face the fate of the old Mission hospital doctors who never got a holiday, year after year. You need many more Binayak Sens, you almost *need* him to be a role model, however difficult that appears to be in today's materialistic, status-driven world, says Sara.

Dr Zachariah is rather more hopeful. He believes that young people are desperately searching for inspirational role models and Binayak fits the bill perfectly. After Jayaprakash Narayan, India has seen no national level social leader, says the professor. His own student Binayak could be that leader, of a much larger people's movement.

As I gently close the gates of Dr Zachariah's bungalow and make my way back to the main CMC hospital building where I want to find my own answers first-hand from the medical students themselves, I think of the burden of expectations that Binayak now carries. Not just from unknown strangers who may quite easily forget tomorrow whatever they are clamouring for today but from his own people who know him well enough to place that burden on his shoulders.

~

Waiting for me patiently, white lab coats slung carelessly over young shoulders, stethoscopes prominently sticking out of pockets, lugging heavy bags and probably heavier schedules, is the jean-clad Gen Next: confident, articulate, analytical.

The first one to speak, George Abraham, is honest about his feelings, "The path Binayak Sen took, it's a very challenging task, at this point I am not sure whether I will take it, I cannot decide now," he says.

Archana says the college made Binayak a role model for all of the students, all of them got to know about him, support him. She may not be able to "do what he did" but his principles appeal to her.

Sara Cherian agrees about the overall nature of the Binayak Sen effect. Simply knowing about him has made them all more sensitive so that if and when they work in urban, commercial areas, all of them will be more sensitive to the issues of the underprivileged.

Shtavin George Paul introduces a more somber note to the discussion, frankly saying that the entire Binayak episode is a deterrent to a lot of people who want to stand up for what is right and fight for civil liberties.

Srujan Sharma disagrees vehemently. For him, Binayak is inspirational, opening up a lot of questions in his mind—is it okay to just be a doctor, to work in a rural hospital? Do students need to go into politics to change the system?

The one common feeling shared by all of them is pride that their alumni stood up so strongly for "one of their own", bolstering their confidence that CMC would do the same for them too, should they choose to follow a similar path.

Will they really want to make similar choices?

Srujan Sharma answers the question head-on. "To be told to be Binayak is a very scary thought. None of us joined medicine to be in the position he was, all of us want happy lives. Nobody wants a life of struggle, nobody wants to be in a situation where you have to stand up for your ideals but my hope is that if I am in such a situation I will react in the way I have been taught to here."

They all have classes to go to and I have already extended my time with them but I find it hard to conclude what has been a unique value-addition to the Binayak Sen story. I restrain myself from asking them why they all unequivocally think Binayak's life has been one of relentless struggle and difficulties and why they don't recognize the happiness and triumphs it contained too.

As I leave Vellore, I drive back to the Big Bungalow Annexe to bid goodbye to the Sens. It is a hot and sleepy afternoon and Pranhita responds to my soft knock on their room door, telling me that everyone is asleep. I leave farewell messages and drive off but an instant later she calls me on my phone, asking me to return. I turn back and find Binayak walking the corridor outside his room. He hugs me and says, "How can you go away from our door without meeting us?"

Once I enter their one-room temporary home, naturally everyone wakes up. I have successfully disturbed their afternoon siesta.

Binayak and Ilina are keen to hear tales about my interaction with the students.

Half an hour later, en route to Chennai in the car, I recall words Binayak used to end his speech while accepting the Paul Harrison award at CMC in 2004: "Neutrality is not a luxury that is available to us. Let us hope we will have the wisdom to choose so that we will be able to live with the choices we have made."

At the same CMC in 2009 I asked him if what he said five years ago still held true. I don't think I need to relate his answer.

Binayak Sen is most definitely and unambiguously living with the choices he made so long ago.

Chapter Four

REACHING OUT THROUGH RUPANTAR

Bagrumnala

I was intensely curious about Ghasiya Ram much before I met him.

The first and rather obvious reason was that Binayak Sen had included him in the list of people who knew him well rather than the more predictable names of well-known people like Arundhati Roy or Anand Patwardhan who publicly supported him during his jail term and continue to do so.

The second reason is a testimony to Binayak's very real, tangible achievements in rural health care over the years.

It takes the form of a story narrated to me by Dr Anurag Bhargava, co-founder of the Jan Swasthya Sahyog (JSS) rural hospital at Ganyari that was also inspired by Binayak Sen. That story too is fascinating and will be shared later, but for now, it is Ghasiya Ram who is the silent, undisputed hero of Anurag's story.

This was the time when Binayak was in jail (May 2007-2009)

and the Ganyari doctors would take turns to run Binayak's Friday clinic at Bagrumnala in Dhamtari district's Nagri block. Binayak's continued absence meant that there were not many patients at the clinic at that time and Anurag suggested to Ghasiya Ram, the health worker left in charge of the Bagrumnala clinic, that they go to the poorest part of the village—to a hamlet where the Khmar tribe lived.

When they reached the hamlet, they saw an eight month old child cradled in the lap of his five-year-old sister. The baby was running a fever, visibly gasping for breath and looked very ill. The mother was not around but everyone in the hamlet seemed to know that the baby was very ill and needed hospitalization. A little later, the mother came and begged the doctors to help.

Anurag asked the mother the baby's name. Before she could reply, Ghasiya Ram said the baby's name was Chandrakant. Since the hamlet comprised 1500 people, Anurag, to be doubly sure, asked the mother the baby's name again. She said, "He *told* you, Chandrakant."

Anurag was impressed. To know the name of an eight month old baby amongst 1500 people requires a very special relationship. *This* was the kind of health worker Binayak had created and trained, someone available, sensitive, responsive to community needs. The baby wasn't just a faceless entity among the thousands that doctors deal with in government clinics.

Anurag and Ghasiya then brought the baby to the clinic, gave him antibiotics and Chandrakant survived! They also arranged for *dal* and *chawal* for him to eat and Ghasiya Ram kept watch over the child and that, Anurag says, is what the real model of health care should be.

You save many more children that way. The UN estimates 2.1 million children in India die before the age of five—four every minute—mostly from preventable diseases such as malaria, typhoid, diarrhoea and pneumonia. UNICEF reports India having the largest number of pneumonia deaths among children in the world, with 2 million children under the age of five dying of this disease each year. Pneumonia is what little Chandrakant had. You need a trained, caring health worker who responds in time.

You need a Ghasiya Ram.

Like Anurag, I am impressed as well and looking forward to meeting Ghasiya Ram and the other health workers who symbolized both the difference *and* the efficacy of the model of rural health care practised and initiated by Binayak Sen.

He's a hard man to find though, Ghasiya Ram. There is no contact telephone or mobile number, no way of getting in touch in advance and Bagrumnala is a village tucked away inside the forests, quite far from the beaten track which is dusty Dhamtari.

My main guide is a disembodied voice over the telephone that belongs to Prahlad Sahu, a coordinator with the Rupantar Trust, the parent organization that runs the clinic amongst a host of other activities. Prahlad is supposed to meet me in Dhamtari so that he can accompany me to Bagrumnala and ensure that villagers talk to me, a complete stranger. He has been unable to get in touch with anyone over the phone to provide them with advance notice as connectivity is non-existent, he informs me apologetically.

When I reach the crowded main road at Dhamtari, Prahlad is nowhere to be seen. His once-again apologetic voice informs me over the mobile phone that he is stuck in Raipur and that I am basically on my own. He gives me some mobile numbers of health workers who may or may not be reachable.

After trying all the numbers in vain, one finally responds. Fortuitously, Phool Singh, health worker, is in Dhamtari right now. He has accompanied a patient from the village, admitted him into hospital and is now free to show me the way to Bagrumnala.

For the next hour or so we talk animatedly about Doc Saab.

Phool Singh is maybe thirty-eight, neatly dressed in formal clothes (probably because he was going to the hospital to get a patient admitted), lean and wiry and articulate. He tells me that the doctor he has just been interacting with at Dhamtari, Dr Dhiren, was commenting on the fact that the number of referral cases had gone down drastically due to Binayak's continued absence from Bagrumnala and that he was sure this would be normalized as soon as the good doctor returned.

It is almost as if the remark from another doctor from a "big hospital" has reassured Phool Singh at some level, even as he makes sure I fully appreciate the public goodwill Binayak has in full measure in this part of the world.

With other doctors in district hospitals, says Phool Singh frankly, you feel a certain hesitation. With Doc Saab this was never there, nobody ever felt that, you could ask him questions without hesitation. Most importantly, he had time for the villagers, visiting Khmar families too, asking people about their financial needs too, and education, apart from nutrition, women's issues like anemia, the 'falciparum' malaria rampant in the area, tuberculosis, other diseases and their cure.

In the year 2000 during a famine when the villagers had little work and no food to eat, Doc Saab helped them with building grain banks. He was one with the villagers in their poverty and suffering, declares Phool Singh emotionally. "I have never seen a man like him, he goes to each and every person's house, asks them about their difficulties, attends to patients in their homes at times, even arranging food for them. Often he would talk to villagers as an assembled bunch, asking them to help out needy people because this is what they should do as a society. He would appeal to other doctors as well when needed. And he never made any distinction between a rich or poor man. If he was invited to a wedding, for example, he would sit on the floor with the villagers and eat with us, like friends!" Phool Singh is clearly an unabashed admirer.

I ask him how long he has known Binayak and am amazed at the answer: nineteen years. Obviously Phool Singh joined Binayak as a young lad, studying in the twin areas of education and health taken up by Rupantar, the voluntary organization set up by Binayak and Ilina, serving the Nagri and Siwaha blocks of Dhamtari district. Though he himself can't have been much older than an adolescent, Phool Singh started off teaching little children in 1996. Later he entered the health sphere, received training from Binayak on TB, about how to make malaria slides. He even went to train for a bit at Shaheed Hospital.

He remembers a time when clinics would be run in three places— in Bagrumnala, Talpara and Gedra. Patients would walk from really far-off places to get to Binayak. They came from Nagri and Kanker, often travelling 30-40 kilometres to reach the doctor. Sometimes the patient-count would touch 100 in a day when "the doctor was in". This being a malaria-prone area, most would come for treatment for malaria but little children would be regulars as well, while the serious cases would be referred to hospitals nearby.

Phool Singh's own favourite tale is the one about an eleven year-old girl who had a bad wound in her chest. She came to Phool Singh for help and he promptly took her to Doc Saab. She was so weak she didn't even look like she was eleven years old. She was diagnosed with TB, treated and cured. In due course she got married but to this day she remembers Doc Saab with gratitude and every time Phool Singh looks at her, he also feels immensely happy that he was able to give her life a new direction by directing her to Binayak.

Describing the more recent trying times when Binayak was in jail, Phool Singh is volubly indignant. Everybody in the area was so angry, they couldn't believe their doctor was in jail! A man who lived with them, ate with them, cured them of their ailments, shared their joys and sorrows, how could *he* be put in jail? Here was a person who used to always talk about how one should always fight for one's rights, and yet he got forcibly framed in this matter, says Phool Singh angrily.

They wanted to meet him in the Central Jail in Raipur but met with staunch opposition. On May 14, 2009, though, many of them travelled to Raipur to take part in the protest rally (the same one that I did) and came back reassured and happy that their doctor was supported by so many people! The day he got bail, two jeep-loads of villagers went to Raipur in joyous celebration.

Phool Singh talks of the harassment faced by all of them after the arrest, in his own particular case, since he handles accounts for Rupantar. The police keep track of him, questioning how he had so much money, questioning his associates about him. Ghasiya too would get rounded up by the police each time there was any minor incident, he adds, his tone now almost resigned.

How did the two-year jail term affect the clinic and the patients in the surrounding villages, I ask him. The Ganyari (Jan Swasthya Sahyog) doctors would come in from Bilaspur and help out, he says, but often they would not be able to make it regularly each week, sometimes the doctors would visit each fortnight, so patients never knew if they would be treated or not, so they would go away disappointed. There's only this much Ghasiya can do after all, he shrugs.

Doc Saab is remembered and missed a lot according to Phool Singh but behind his wistful words and his sentiments lies an equally unshakeable belief that Binayak will be back in Bagrumnala with all of them one day. Till that day, they will all continue doing what he has taught them to do. They will keep the faith.

I am humbled by the staunchness of that faith but no longer surprised by it. This has by now, become a familiar refrain. As we continue to talk about Binayak Sen and his links with people in the Nagri block where the clinic is situated, Phool Singh suddenly asks the driver to stop the car. His sharp eyes have spotted what I can only describe as God's small way of helping me out, another fortuitous event—all the people I want and need to meet are gathered together for a cultural function at a forest community hall, on the left of the road.

Music is blaring forth from loudspeakers, gaily dressed women with flowers in their hair and men in sparkling white *dhoti-kurtas* are just finishing a late lunch. Suraj Singh Netam, Bhukauram Kunjam, Baniram Guru—health workers along with the elusive Ghasiya Ram are all present here, hopefully with more information for me. Phool Singh does the honours, introducing me and my mission, and willingly they all sit down in the garden to share stories about their doctor.

I request Ghasiya Ram to accompany me to Bagrumnala clinic and he too readily agrees, and settles down to listen to his colleagues for the moment. At my urging, the raucous music is lowered for a while and we begin talking about the Binayak effect. But here it's not just the Binayak effect at play. The influence, the credit, the triumphs are jointly shared by Binayak and Ilina, since it's not just medicine that was practised in these twenty-six villages.

Bhukauram Kunjam, a Rupantar health worker sums it up succinctly. "For the first time in our lives, we read a book in Chhattisgarhi language and I can't tell you how good it felt," he says, talking about a time when there was no school in their village, not for children and certainly not for adults! Adult education was a totally alien concept for villagers but it really caught on and soon transformed even the children's education programmes, courtesy Didi (Ilina) and Doc Saab's direction, he says proudly. He estimates an improvement of a record 80 per cent in the area's villages over the last decade and a half in the fields of education and medicine.

Suraj Singh Netam, another health worker, nods in agreement. He too has known and worked closely with the Sens for a long period. He puts the figure at 75 per cent and we all laugh at the reduction of 5 per cent, embarrassing him hugely. He hastens to tell me how much he admires Binayak and always has, not just for the community initiatives he launched but because he never takes any decision unilaterally. He always asks the opinions of the entire community at large, discussing pros and cons.

The change isn't just in the nature or volume of work done in this area, whether it was the considerable reduction of the rampant and deadly 'falciparum' malaria or effective and timely treatment of tuberculosis (a life-long concern with Binayak) or the establishment of schools for children and adult education classes. The change isn't in the increased awareness about health or social issues either. The change is in the mindset, in people's ways of thinking and *that* is the biggest victory of them all.

Don't discriminate, behave the same way with everyone: that is the dictum that was taught by example and that is what has seeped in and is being articulated with pride today. Bani Ramguru of Kera village, also a health worker, says simply, "I learnt to heal patients, to talk to them politely, with dignity because I saw Doc Saab doing the same. Even when he shared a meal with us, he would serve others, not wait to be served."

They also learnt to overcome stubborn views on injections and tablets and syrups, ultimately recognizing the wisdom of Binayak's warnings through continued contact and benefit, courtesy the clinic.

In the early days before the Rupantar clinics were started in this region, villagers would go to city doctors who would pay scant attention to them, scribble something on a scrap of paper and charge an exorbitant amount of money for services rendered. Hospitalization and expensive medical investigative procedures in city referral centres would often wipe off as much as a villager's year's savings. Once the Rupantar clinics began however, the doctor would take time over a patient, then give tablets worth not more than Rs 40-50 and initially the patients would scoff, "What kind of a doctor is this? He doesn't even give an injection!" But then, slowly and steadily, as people got cured day after day, and patients found they were spending Rs 200 instead of Rs 2,000 they realized the kind of doctor they were dealing with. Knowledge about the side effects and after-effects of over-use of injections helped them understand and later oppose their indiscriminate use. Learning about common ailments like cold and cough, the efficacy of a 50 paise paracetamol tablet instead of a Rs 30 injection armed them against being duped or misled.

A doctor who asks people for their suggestions, thinks them over and then offers an opinion, was rather special. And this is why, when people in these parts heard of the chargesheet against Binayak, that he was accused of being a "fake doctor", they told the police in no uncertain terms that he was in fact a family member in addition to being their doctor!

Do they all believe he will return to their area? I ask, even as I prepare to leave with Ghasiya Ram for Bagrumnala. Of course he will, they chorus loudly in reply, their confidence rock-solid.

~

Ghasiya Ram and I drive through a "black-top" or tarred road that is flanked on both sides by lush green trees, dappled sunlight peeking through leaves here and there, blinding me from time to time. For almost forty-five minutes now the road is virtually empty except for a stray villager walking along with a stick. In the distance one can even hear cowbells since it is nearing the magic hour of dusk.

It is a drive that soothes one's spirit, calming and enriching it at the same time. You can almost feel unnecessary tensions melt away. In some uncanny, unspoken communication, Ghasiya Ram and I share the silence and the peace. In any case, he is extremely shy and quiet, or at least gives the appearance of being so, a near-invisible presence while the other health workers were talking about the clinic he is in charge of today.

As a sign proclaiming Bagrumnala's identity looms ahead, Ghasiya asks the driver to turn off into the dirt road. We are going to meet Prem Bai first, he says hesitantly, she may not be available later. Her village, Kekrakholi, is on the way and since she too is on that same list given to me by Binayak—of people who know him well and whom he respects in turn—I agree with Ghasiya's suggestion.

Prem Bai is perhaps in her late forties, simply clad in a sari, embellished with gold earrings, a gold nose-stud and red bangles. Her pleasant face is warm and welcoming. As usual the name "Binayak Sen" works like the magic mantra it is in this part of the world. She has never met me or heard of me but invoking the doctor's name is quite enough for her to usher me into her hut and her family. A couple of small, bright-eyed children run around us and I am unsure whose children they are and they watch me equally curiously.

A *charpoy* is immediately fetched for me to sit on despite my protests that the spiffy clean floor will do just as well. I insist that she sit facing me, her gentle voice is so low that I have to strain to hear her words. Her much-older looking husband (I assume he is her husband more from his demeanour rather than an actual introduction) is sprawled behind us on another *charpoy*, interjecting his own comments, unasked, from time to time. Ghasiya watches in familiar silence from a corner of the open courtyard where we are all seated.

She speaks in heavily-accented Chhattisgarhi Hindi but I manage to understand her fairly well, her face is quite mobile, changing expression frequently. She also smiles often, a large toothy grin that serves as a response for questions she is too shy to answer. In a unique feat of achievement, Prem Bai had been the *sarpanch* of Bagrumnala, elected unopposed, for ten long years.

When I marvel at this, asking her about this goodwill earned no doubt due to good work done, she is unassuming and modest. Instead she talks of how Binayak Sen taught her to form small groups of women workers in villages, on the lines of self-help groups. Initially the women groups had little money of their own, slowly they gathered funds and support and now are able to sustain themselves.

She also reiterates (like others before her) how the doctor guided them during the famine, told them to store rice in grain banks. Promoting grain biodiversity and organic farming and sustainable livelihood schemes for income generation for women self help groups were other major milestones of Rupantar's achievements. More than anything else, the women's way of thinking changed, she says softly. Binayak advised them about different ways of earning a livelihood. In the beginning they could not implement his suggestions fully since they had to work in the fields but bit by bit, they got involved with health work, with education, with the mid-day meal scheme, with society at large. It is the familiar holistic Binayak Sen effect again, reminiscent of the model followed in Dalli Rajahara. Health work not done in isolation but combined with an understanding of community needs.

Prem Bai herself interacted the most with Binayak, helping him find and set up the clinic at Bagrumnala in 1997–98. She is extremely proud of the reputation that the clinic built up over the years, with long queues of patients traveling long distances to keep their weekly appointment with Binayak Sen.

Her own personal story about the doctor is a deeply emotional one and she openly says she will never forget what she and her family owe Binayak. Her husband nods vigorously behind her but thankfully does not interrupt at this juncture. She talks of how her seven year old son Ganganand was extremely ill, diagnosed with a heart condition and advised an operation that the family could not afford. Binayak approached the District Collector, got the funds, cured her boy of his problem. Binayak even arranged for them to go to Delhi for an operation, she says almost with awe. Later Ganganand had malaria which was successfully treated and today he is fine.

The doctor has treated every member of her family she says, has helped them all so much, he is family to them, visiting their home during his weekly visits to the clinic. The best quality about Binayak Sen is his behaviour, she says shyly, looking at her husband behind her for reassurance, which he provides vigorously. Doc Saab treats rich and poor alike (anyone heard this before?), sits on the floor, actually cares about a poor person's problems.

But he's not a serious person, he's a very happy person, she clarifies, repeating the statement, much to my amusement.

How is he, she asks me in turn. "I haven't seen him in so long, almost three years. I did go to the May 14, 2009 protest rally in Raipur, along with five other women from the village. We all shouted slogans protesting against his arrest and asking for his release. Everyone remembers and asks after him here. The number of patients at the clinic has naturally declined. Patients still come to Bagrumnala clinic and ask us when he is coming back. Is he in, is he out? But nobody has an answer." Prem Bai looks woe-begone, quite bereft while saying this. Ghasiya looks on in solemn agreement.

It is now almost sunset and, declining her hospitable offer of tea, Ghasiya and I make our way towards the Bagrumnala clinic that has been spoken about with so much pride. En route we literally bump into Ganganand, fifteen or sixteen years old today, cycling past us, radiating health and a bit embarrassed when his mother Prem Bai points this out to me emphatically..."See, he's absolutely fine now..."

~

Bagrumnala is a village like any other, thatched-roof huts with red tiles, mud walls with chalk scribbles on them, a hand-pump in the centre of the village, a stray tractor discarded in a corner. Women drawing water, walking away carrying vessels on their heads.

The somewhat overcast sky does not prevent me from appreciating the pure fresh air, the open vista, green fields and well-endowed trees that are the fringe benefits of life in rural India. So is the lack of noise, the intrusive cacophony that pounds one's ears and senses in cities. Here the sounds are gentle—a hand-pump being pulled rhythmically, children's voices indistinguishable in content yet part of the ambience, as are their school uniforms, common all over the country, blue pinafores or shorts and white shirts. Chickens cluck in the background. Occasionally a jarring note sounds, with a motor-cyclist roaring past, laden with goods to sell.

I soak it all in.

And then I look for Binayak's clinic. At first glance one could even miss it if it wasn't for the words "Mitanin" scribbled on the walls of the thatched-roof structure.

Ironically, this Mitanin (the word means "friend" in the Chhattisgarhi language) community health worker scheme is a government sponsored one, freely advertised on the walls of Binayak's clinic. On closer inspection, I also make out the word Rupantar written in pink chalk in Hindi. Census notations and sundry information such as "*Kusht rog ki jaanch kijiye*" (Get yourself tested for leprosy) adorn the walls of the clinic too.

Ghasiya Ram unlocks the clinic and shows me around. It is a modest four or five room brick-tiled structure, the windows at the entrance are barred, there is an L-shaped sitting area along the sides of the walls of what is obviously a waiting room. Walking past it, through the small door, the open courtyard seems more spacious, with overhanging trees, a black Sintex water drum in a corner, several steel buckets lying face down, a few plastic mugs and a broom in a corner.

I start walking in and out of empty rooms, trying to visualize them as they might have been when the clinic was fully functional with Binayak in attendance every Friday. His personal room where he sometimes spent the night if the patients over-ran or if there was extra work is typically spartan, with one iron bed, a rolled up thin cotton mattress and an equally typical inspirational calendar on the wall. The calendar actually has an old photograph of a bearded Binayak holding a smiling baby in his arms, watched fondly by Ilina and Sudha Bhardwaj, both wearing equally beaming smiles. The Kofi Annan quotation at the bottom of the calendar sums up the philosophy of the clinic and its doctor: "It is my aspiration that health will finally be seen not as a blessing to be wished for but as a human right to be fought for."

Ghasiya Ram leads me to the main "Doctor room" where currently he holds fort in Binayak's place. It's fairly small, just above the standard desk and chair is a window covered with *chattai*, there is just enough light peeking through the bars to give me a glimpse of two huts opposite the clinic with the village beyond. A small hole in the roof provides a natural sky light, glinting rays of the setting sun enter the room sneakily. A steel cupboard, slotted angle shelves stacked with medicines, syringes, injections, tubes, syrup bottles jostling for space along with a wooden chair with no backrest on which some kind of medical equipment is kept. Another old shelf of slotted iron angles, heaped full with large bottles of medicine and an empty Bisleri bottle complete the room's basic amenities.

Ghasiya and I move to the empty adjacent room (where there is only a bare iron bed without even a mattress), to talk about the absent occupant of the "Doctor room". They still come, says Ghasiya wonderingly, some from places as far away as 30 kilometres, in the hope that he can cure them. Every day they ask when their doctor will return. They think of him as God, trust him implicitly, firmly believing that if they are examined by him they will feel better.

In a somewhat unfair comparison he tells me that when the Ganyari (Jan Swasthya Sahyog, Bilaspur) doctors would visit the clinic in Binayak's absence to fill in for him, patients would tell Ghasiya, "We will be cured only when *our* doctor comes and gives us the tablets." So it's principally a trust issue, I say. Medicines and trust, Ghasiya says solemnly.

Ghasiya has by now, after spending some four-odd hours quietly observing me talk to other health workers about Binayak, decided to trust me, in turn. Quite shy so far, he unbends enough to share stories and not just about his boss, Binayak.

Ghasiya Ram is forty years old, short, wiry, speaks quite confidently and displays rare humour at times. I start by telling him how well he is regarded by Binayak and he smiles in pleasure, clearly taken aback at my opening statement. Ghasiya has trained as a health worker with Binayak whom he has known and interacted with since 1994. He also learnt the ropes from the trained lab technician Lilu working at Bagrumnala, later receiving formal training for malaria detection through the use of slides in hospital labs in Bilaspur.

Even though Rupantar ran two other clinics earlier, it was the Bagrumnala clinic that lasted the longest and made the strongest mark. Even today all that is needed is for the clinic's doctor to be re-united with his patients and the remarkable success story will begin all over again. Waiting as patiently and eagerly for that day, Ghasiya Ram shares with me memories of his days, more specifically, Fridays!

That was the designated day of the week for Binayak to travel down from Raipur, first to Dhamtari around 80 kilometres away, and then onwards to Bagrumnala, a further 35 odd kilometres, but on wobbly roads, so his total travel time each week was anywhere between three and three-and-a-half hours. He would get in by noon, immediately start seeing the long queues of waiting patients, assisted by Ghasiya and other health workers who would dole out the medicines he prescribed. The only fees accepted was for medicines, and for the backward and BPL (Below Poverty Line) Khmar tribe even those were free! The more serious patients would be sent for referrals to Dhamtari. Transport would be arranged for them by the clinic's workers.

On a regular Friday, the average patient count would be between 50-75, since the clinic actually served almost 247 villages! Understandably therefore, despite the doctor's skill and experience and quick diagnosis, lunch times would get delayed. The food, simple *dal-sabzi*, was cooked by the workers at the clinic and everyone ate together. Binayak would eat whatever was placed in front of him, simultaneously discussing different issues related to village problems, offering suggestions for "better living", says Ghasiya.

People from villages are often given the run-around by officials so Binayak would intervene on their behalf, speak to the local MLA. Ghasiya recalls him procuring a rice machine once for Bagrumnala.

Post-lunch, the OPD would begin again and go on till late evening. Sometimes if it got too late or if there were health or government-related problems to be sorted out, he would stay the night.

Most importantly, Binayak would impart to villagers basic knowledge about health, make them aware of illnesses so that they wouldn't need to run around wasting valuable money on quacks and unnecessary injections. "A simple thing like blood pressure, for example, Doc Saab would tell patients if you have high BP you will need tablets all your life. Even for TB, he would tell us, get monthly check-ups done, this clinic cured lots of TB patients. The Directly Observed Therapy Short Course or DOTS programme of the government came much later," clarifies Ghasiya.

In the most sincere form of admiration, Ghasiya has tried to emulate Binayak. His face lights up while telling me the story, becoming animated and flushed with pride. "Doc Saab is a person who treats everyone alike, anyone who has a problem and comes to him, he talks to them very nicely and in detail, empathizing with them. I tried to learn this empathizing with peoples' suffering. There was a Khmar man who was severely ill with pneumonia. You had to constantly monitor him, give him his medicines, feed him. He would not do it on his own. So I tended to him, made *khichdi* for him, fed him, gave him medicines and then he got better. I told Doc Saab about this and he praised me!"

Today Ghasiya is the only health worker still accessible to the villagers in the Bagrumnala clinic but on Binayak's instructions, he does not take on any new cases, merely referring to old prescriptions and giving medicines where required or referring serious patients to hospitals. Since he can prepare slides for malaria detection, he treats that as well if the slide is positive. "People get reassured when I show them the slides, they believe me," he says simply. But clearly he is only filling time, he knows that, the patients waiting for Binayak know that, if only the people who kept the doctor away from his people knew that as well!

Ghasiya speaks of the harassment faced with an amused smile, making much less of it than it must have been. "A jeep came here, policemen entered the clinic and started searching for God knows what…they asked me to show them the records of patients which I did. Then they asked me, why are there so many mattresses? (laughs). Then they asked me, what are these medicines? The *thanedar* even asked me to check his BP. Perhaps he wanted to see if I knew my job! Finally they went away. But at that time (two years ago) they used to keep a watch on the people who came to the clinic and the villagers would tell them in turn that they got treated here!"

The day Binayak got bail—May 25, 2009—Ghasiya Ram was undergoing training in Bilaspur. Binayak told him over the phone to learn properly because he was coming back and they would be starting the clinic again. Those few words are enough for Ghasiya to tell me firmly, "I know the clinic will start functioning fully again. The nurses will be sent for training, we need nurses for delivery cases. Till then I am holding fort."

I leave Ghasiya, a small, silhouetted figure standing alone outside the clinic as the sun sets finally, the swirling dust thrown up by the car blocking my last view of the two—the clinic and its caretaker. My curiosity has been fully assuaged, replaced by immense respect for all the community health workers who represent Rupantar and the Sens in this area. They are the real keepers of the faith Binayak and Ilina have reposed in them.

~

Once again, in continuation of the collaborative spirit of the Dalli Rajhara days, it is the concept of community that is paramount both in the conceptualization and implementation of Rupantar's health programme. All the health workers are part of the community, bonding personally with their patients, so the process of healing takes place in a context. Binayak is insistent on this, saying that if you remove the context, then the entire process of healing is actually denied, the convivial ethos that healing has to have is not there if the community is taken away from the healing process.

Often doctors themselves are not seen as being part of this community healing, they are considered too technical, even the kindest of them and so you need a nexus. Binayak tried to foster that nexus with the health workers and also with the patients, by sharing medical knowledge, by demystifying medical jargon. Medicine, says Binayak, is largely viewed by people as another version of esoteric magic, which is very sad because then the liberating scientific aspect of medical knowledge is completely destroyed. It becomes simply yet another black box invention. A doctor opens his box, takes something out, gives it to the patient and the patient gets better.

The whole idea of how a disease is diagnosed and treated is woefully lacking, he claims. There is an urgent need to develop a scientific attitude in society because one of the commonest forms of science that people have access to is medicine. But if the knowledge has to be liberating knowledge then people need to know what is happening. This is what he tried to do over the years in Bagrumnala with the health workers whom he describes as "extremely efficient" during his weekly visits which were "like clockwork".

Their health-worker based programme of diagnosis and treatment for malaria, for example, worked really well, he says with unaccustomed satisfaction. The Nagri-Siwaha area was endemic for 'falciparum' and 'vivax' malaria and what the government primary health centres, or PHCs, used to do was simply distribute chloroquine tablets to people if they complained of fever, that too in insufficient doses.

As part of Rupantar, Binayak taught the health workers to diagnose malaria from slides, he set up a slide examination centre, worked out the logistics of having the slides examined and getting the reports ready within twenty-four hours and in this way, people were able to treat malaria in a scientific manner, thereby reducing the impact of the disease significantly in those communities.

Binayak also mentions setting up a diagnosis and treatment centre for TB which later had to be shut down when the government introduced the DOTS programme with different criteria for lab requirements.

The low cost of medicines at the clinics run by Rupantar are courtesy colleagues like Baroda-based Chinu Shrivastava who provide drugs at cheap rates specifically for progressive health professionals, for projects run by hospitals. These drugs are not available on the open market, clarifies Binayak.

I ask him why, despite the careful building up and nurturing of a community health care system with caring, dedicated health workers over the years, he seems irreplaceable at the Bagrumnala clinic.

It has been over four months since he is out on bail (at the time I have returned from Bagrumnala and am talking to Binayak) but Ilina's illness has prevented him from getting back to work at the clinic. He is distressed and grieved to learn that patients have more or less dwindled to an average of seven per week from the earlier fifty-four (figure given by Ganyari) and that the health workers who were supposed to have taken over, are not quite instilling the same confidence in the villagers as he did.

So is it true then, that a doctor in a village cannot be replaced as easily as perhaps a doctor in an institution like the All India Institute of Medical Sciences (AIIMS) or CMC? He thinks long and hard before replying, "Medicine cannot be run by a bureaucracy, where you have replaceable elements. But you have to have a mixture of both, you have to have a turnover, otherwise you cannot have individuals giving their lives and then they are not related to the rest of the profession. That cannot be the case."

It may not be quite the answer Ghasiya Ram and the people of the 246 villages that were served by the Bagrumnala clinic want to hear but it is the only one that Binayak has at the moment.

Ilina echoes the uncertainty of the future of the Friday clinics. "We are now trying to re-build, to upgrade into a network of health worker-based clinics because we are not sure when we can go back," she says. "We are also not sure about how viable it will be for Binayak to continue to work in that area because the government is still after him. Let's see how it goes. Many of our senior health workers are not very happy with the state of the Mitanin programme, so if at all we are able to synergize organization then many of our senior health workers will come back to us. JSS (Ganyari doctors) is supposed to train them."

She emphasizes that moving to the Bagrumnala area was a very conscious decision. There was a revolt called the *Lal Topi andolan* in the area around forty years ago by people who had been displaced by dams (built on the Mahanadi river), many of whom then encroached into forests. This (*Lal Topi*) movement led to

At school in Calcutta

Binayak during JNU days

Binayak during his graduation from Christian Medical College, Vellore

Binayak with the first batch of health workers he trained, Rasulia 1980

Binayak with his father at home in Kalyani

Binayak at the wedding of then CMM colleague, Shekh Ansar

Binayak and Ilina at home at Tilda

During a PUCL factfinding with advocate HL Prajapati, Dhamtari in the 1990s

The building of Shaheed hospital, a truly collective enterprise by the workers of Dalli Rajhara

the setting up of Malgaons or illegal settlements in forest areas, demanding recognition as villages. This is how the Gond tribals settled elsewhere too, she says. The Indian state does not recognize this process, hence such settlers face enormous difficulties, their fields are burnt, their houses broken into. The government broke down five of the original eighteen Malgaons but the remaining thirteen were a challenge for the Sens. So they started setting up schools or educational centres in these thirteen villages, in some cases beginning with older learners, in others with children.

Ilina recalls that when they first began the educational centres in the Malgaons, they began with literally nothing. Since the state did not recognize that they existed at all, there was no electricity, no land rights, no health centres and no schools. Ultimately Rupantar established a school in a small place called Kekrakholi in 1992 which later became a residential school with children from all the neighbouring villages enrolling in it. Built from scratch by the villagers, it was on their own land. Later when the hostel was started, the villagers built that themselves too. Parents of the children contributed in kind, sometimes with rice grain, sometimes by working on the land. Cash was a very rare contribution, smiles Ilina in memory.

Fund raising must have been a major issue, I comment. Yes, it was, she says. Rupantar went in for a long-term partnership with ActionAid, one of their major donors. Despite the accompanying bureaucracy, Rupantar managed to retain its original ethos, never professionalizing its staff, in fact never using that word "staff". They call them *saathins* or friends.

After running the schools successfully for almost eleven years, when the Sarva Shiksha Abhiyaan was launched and government schools came into the villages, Rupantar withdrew, not wanting villagers to be conflicted. In a small village, if there were to be a government school and a Rupantar school, each vying with the other, duplicating, competing for favours, it would have destroyed the village cohesion and hence, one by one, first the smaller schools shut down and at the very end, in 2003 when the government school came up in Kekrakholi, the residential Rupantar school shut down as well, the last one to do so.

Ilina and Binayak had several interactions with the Kekrakholi villagers who wanted them to stay on to run the middle school, with the government running the primary school, but they ultimately took the painful decision to not do so.

A decade of unique effort came to an end.

The Bagrumnala clinic remained.

Binayak and Ilina were invited to be on the state advisory committee to implement structural reforms in health care which the Chhattisgarh government had initiated, with the Mitanin programme as an integral component, giving the Sens access to the entire health care system in the two blocks of Nagri and Magarlod. Ironically, the Mitanin programme later adversely affected the Bagrumnala clinic as more and more health workers began referring patients to the government PHCs. Bagrumnala became a stand-alone initiative, still very popular due to word-of-mouth appreciation, due to Doc Saab.

But then in May 2007 the doctor was arrested and labelled a "fake doctor" and his clinic stood alone again, as it does today.

The road to Bagrumnala may continue to be a bumpy one for Binayak in more ways than one, but does that mean it may be a road not taken at all? The answer to that question lies in the unflinching belief shining in Ghasiya Ram's eyes and on the faces of all the people I met in Bagrumnala who told me with no uncertainty, "Doc Saab will be back with us soon".

Chapter Five

TAKING THE LEGACY FORWARD

Ganyari

How many people are fortunate enough to inspire genuine feelings of emulation, of respect, of admiration, in their own lifetime? The answer to that question lies in the distance from the Bagrumnala clinic to the one I am now making my way to—the Jan Swasthya Sahyog, Ganyari. The auto-rickshaw driver quotes Rs 500 for the hour's drive to Ganyari, promising to wait and bring me back to Bilaspur in the evening to catch the train back to Raipur. Since it seems extremely reasonable and also because there is no alternative, I embark on what proves to be a very rickety ride across truly bad roads.

What transforms the entire hour however is the scenic beauty once you are out of Bilaspur's bustling streets. The road, though full of pot-holes and dug up in many spots, is flanked by lush greenery on both sides, rural India shining at its very best, rain and fierce winds bearing down on my delighted face. Hence the smile that stays with me through the day.

It isn't necessary to ask for directions once we reach Ganyari. All I have to do is say "hospital" and in minutes I am deposited in front of the Jan Swasthya Sahyog (JSS), a "people-centric community-based model of health care" as described in its brochure. What the brochure does *not* mention is what I observe for the next five hours in quiet admiration. In all my years of reporting as a journalist, especially covering primary health centres across the country, I have never seen such empathetic patient care in a rural hospital.

But this is no ordinary hospital and these are not ordinary doctors.

Dr Anurag Bhargava and Dr Yogesh Jain are the two names given to me by Binayak Sen, and I enter the modest, thatched-roof, single-storeyed premises of JSS looking for them. Both have been informed about my visit and the reasons behind it, through telephone conversations and predictably, both of them are not free!

As I wend my way through incredibly long queues of patients thronging the hospital's various OPDs, I prepare myself for a long wait. It is no hardship at all. There are at least five or six human stories unfolding in front of me simultaneously but before I can absorb them, Dr Anurag Bhargava, tall, forty-ish with premature grey flecks in a short hair-style, armed with a stethoscope and a welcoming smile, is standing in front of me, apologetic about the delay in our appointment on account of his many waiting patients. It will take at least a couple of hours to see them all, he says, why don't I meet Yogesh in the meantime? He helps me with my various bags and umbrella, walking with me to Yogesh's office till I protest about his waiting patients. He then assigns a health worker to be my guide and plunges back into his crowded domain.

I walk past jostling patients, almost all villagers laden with heavy, bulging bags, hospital files in hand, varying degrees of anxiety on their faces, some of them seated on the ground outside the crowded corridors, resigned to a long wait.

I reach a modest office furnished sparsely with the requisite doctor's table and chair, the only difference being the fresh air coming in through the windows overlooking benign, flowering trees outside. The room is empty. The health worker tells me Dr Yogesh Jain is on a field visit to a nearby village and will be back shortly.

Almost an hour later, he rushes in, explaining that the visit lasted longer than expected, offers me tea and takes a deep breath to settle down.

Dr Yogesh Jain has MBBS and MD degrees from India's prestigious AIIMS in Delhi, he is winner of a National Merit scholarship, National Talent Search scholarship, AIIMS scholarship for second rank in MBBS, best undergraduate student in community medicine, best post-graduate student in paediatrics (his chosen speciality), former Assistant Professor in the Paediatrics Department of AIIMS.

Now, simply known as Community Doctor in JSS, Ganyari.

He is perhaps forty-five, looks younger despite the slightly greying hair, and I recall seeing him earlier, both at A-26 Surya Apartments in Raipur (Binayak's home) and at the May 14, 2009 rally to demand Binayak's release from prison. "I have a very common face, people are always telling me they saw me somewhere," he laughs.

Over the next one hour he is alternately analytical, cynical, unflinchingly honest and remarkably passionate about rural health care and the model of medicine that is best prescribed for it. He begins on a personal note, in part to satisfy my curiosity. "When we first came to Ganyari and started JSS in 1989, my mother used to say you will only treat children with colds in such a place. But our logic was that at AIIMS, if you were not there, someone else was there to replace you. Out here there is no one to replace us. We feel far more challenged, academically challenged, we have learnt a huge amount. Also, one needs to be far more technically competent out here, its not like it's a small place therefore the problems are small too."

Is that another fallacy, that you don't need expertise in dealing with villagers, *gaon mein sab chalta hai?* I ask him. Yes, he agrees, people have a lot of fallacies, lots of myths. The truth is that issues of providing good quality health care in a place like Ganyari are far more complex.

This after all, was their combined vision, to combat their collective dissatisfaction over the technocentric, hospital-based vision of tertiary health care. Setting up base in a rural area, involving and empowering village communities in preventing and treating illness, evolving low-cost technology and curative service to address public health problems in rural areas with appropriate solutions...all of this is delineated in the philosophy of JSS and its team of doctors.

A decade since it was set up, JSS has on board two paediatricians, a paediatric surgeon, two physicians, a gynaecologist, an ENT surgeon, an Ayurvedic physician, an epidemiologist, a research chemist and two public health physicians. The rest of the team comprising village programme coordinators, nurses, pharmacists, paramedical professionals and people in support functions, numbers a total of 100 personnel.

I am intensely curious about why such a highly qualified paediatrician from one of the country's premier institutions chose to pursue his vocation in a rural outpost in Chhattisgarh. Dr Yogesh Jain provides a detailed and remarkable analysis of not just the setting up of JSS but also an overview of how the medical profession operates. He explains this to me without using medical jargon.

There are three types of good doctors, he says.

The Type-1 doctor is one who heals body and mind, does a good diagnosis, provides the correct and rational treatment, choosing cheap yet effective drugs, giving his patient both an explanation and ensuring good follow-up. If you consider public health as a summation of health concerns of individuals, such doctors contribute to public health as well. Yogesh counts several friends in good hospitals in Delhi and elsewhere as the Type-1 doctor doing good work.

The Type-2 doctor looks not only at the illness but also at the determinant of the illness. If it's a water borne disease, for example, he will ensure that safe drinking water is provided, make better programmes, campaign for rational drugs, price control drugs, for preventive strategies for illness to reduce costs. Many of the public health institutions and medical colleges come under this category, they look at the proximate causes of health and manage them. Doctors at JSS, Ganyari, a vast majority of them, are Type-2 doctors, maybe half a stage higher, says Yogesh.

When you start looking at root causes, and working on those, that is not the sanitized part of public health. No public health institution or medical college will teach you why investment in developing rural India is less, or how people who are victims of displacement or violence are supposed to get their due of good health, whether they should ask questions that are directly political and link ill health to politics, to inequity of distribution of resources, whether it is water or food or money or health care services. Health work of this kind is a political act, and this is the Type-3 doctor.

Binayak Sen, says Yogesh, is a Type-3 doctor.

In the overall scheme of things a person can be a Type-1 doctor fighting inequity in a limited way, he can be a Type-2 doctor continuing the same in a more advanced though cautious way, *and* he can be a Type-3 doctor who does not care about consequences, actively does political work and has the "balls" to go ahead.

Yogesh Jain is honest enough to say that even though he considers Binayak's work to be a logical extension of public health work (unlike the majority of the medical fraternity which did not understand it as such), he himself may not be very comfortable doing it. He thinks of himself as contributing significantly in the Type-2 doctor's mould, even while admitting that of course that is not adequate and someone has to do the Type-3 doctor's work.

"So, you would admire the Type-3 doctor?" I query.

"Yes, I do. I admire Binayak because I can't do it myself, and I would support someone who does! Actually at JSS we do more than just the Type-2 doc's work...we do question policies and have some understanding about poor people and to our own extent we are trying to sort it out. But not in the way Binayak did."

This in fact is a common refrain I have heard from different people who are close to Binayak Sen, admiration for Binayak coupled with the honest admission that they wish they could be like him. With every new person who echoes this sentiment, my impressions of just how difficult Binayak's work and stances must have been, are strengthened.

I ask Yogesh about the bond with Binayak, if he is their mentor, their inspiration and he immediately nods in agreement. "Part of our reason for moving to Chhattisgarh was based on the fact that Binayak was working in another part of Chhattisgarh. We came to know him as a public health person through the Medico

Friends Circle, a close group of health professionals trying to develop an alternative vision of health care. From then on, one has been in touch with him, trying to learn things from him. This friendship and his guidance allowed us to plan this work in Ganyari together. Though he has not been working here he is a part of the board since the beginning, sharing so many ideas, we have grown together and in that sense, Binayak has been very much part of this work even though in a physical sense his health care work is more in the districts of Dhamtari, Durg and Raipur."

Yogesh also describes Binayak as a keen listener, someone who raises good questions and offers good solutions to issues to be tackled as part of their process in Ganyari. Raising pertinent questions about improvement in children's health care or accessing health care for the rural poor, including as many people as possible in trying to answer those questions, learning from anyone rather than highlighting himself...these are some of Binayak's key characteristics, according to Yogesh, who emphasizes that Binayak is far more of a "process person" than a "personality person".

And this is why you won't hear his name being highlighted in the health care of tribals or malaria eradication or tuberculosis treatment unlike many doctors who contribute far less but manage to garner a lion's share of the limelight that often accompanies those working with inequity, says Yogesh, mincing no words.

~

The year 2010 marks a decade of JSS work in rural Bilaspur, the voluntary, non-profit registered society of health professionals running a low-cost health programme for the tribal and rural poor through a community health programme and a hospital.

The sheer volume of work done over the years is staggering. Here are the statistics:

o Early diagnosis and prompt treatment of malaria

o The JSS out-patient clinic at Ganyari, complete with a dispensary, radiology and laboratory services, has provided more than 3.5 lakh consultations to over 150,000 patients drawn from more than 15,000 villages and towns of Chhattisgarh and adjoining districts of eastern Madhya Pradesh.

o An in-patient ward with 35 beds and an operation theatre has dispensed surgical services to more than 17,000 patients.

o Three sub-centres in three forest village clusters, about 45-75 kilometres from Bilaspur town, serve 150 forest and forest-fringe villages through senior health workers supported by doctor-based outreach clinics each week.

o A community health programme provides preventive and curative services through 104 trained village health workers, elected by their respective villages, in 53 tribal villages.

Far, *far* more importantly, the quality of health care provided at JSS has to be seen to be understood and appreciated. The overflowing queues of patients only adds to the dedicated urgency of the doctors who serve them, there is no sense of hurry, everyone is attended to politely and gently. Their "token" system facilitates efficiency as well as the follow-up protocol and above all, patients' questions are addressed seriously and answered in full.

To a person in pain, not knowing what is wrong or how long it will take for the illness to be cured and myriad other related worries, a doctor who listens and provides solutions is akin to God and not surprisingly I watch patients at the Ganyari hospital treat the doctors as their saviours. Which to a very real extent they are!

I watch a lady doctor gently steer an old man who comes up repeatedly to her with a sample bottle, reassuring him that his test is to be done the following day. Her patience does not wear thin, neither does her voice with each repetition of the old man's wandering trips. In an OPD of more than 250 patients daily, feeling and exhibiting empathy is no mean task.

"Who is accompanying you? How will you get home?" are regular questions asked of the patients here. The follow-up care is genuine and rarely found in urban health centres, in fact, even in any of the rural health centres run by state governments that I have visited over twenty years, and this, once again, confirms my belief that this is no ordinary hospital.

They use innovative techniques like making school children couriers for malaria slides, delivered from the health care worker in a remote village to the child on his way to school, to the bus conductor of the solitary bus that plies that route daily, to the hospital that delivers the report back via the same route, the same evening! Thus expediting both the diagnosis and treatment of malaria in far-off, forgotten villages.

This early one-day diagnosis based on slides was what worked best at Binayak's Bagrumnala clinic as well, going a long way towards controlling the spread of malaria.

The JSS team went on to demonstrate to me five things that a rural clinic can do which a city hospital cannot do:

o   Early diagnosis and prompt treatment of malaria

o   Early diagnosis of tuberculosis

o   Easy access in terms of distance. Villagers doing farm work, children, old people, pregnant women—will all prefer going to a village clinic rather than a city one or a referral hospital. If there is no clinic at a reasonable distance of a few kilometres, they will suffer silently or decide against treatment.

o Manage animal bites as a significant problem—this is one of the commonest forms of death and disability in rural India and it remains poorly recorded as such, with public health systems ignoring this health hazard, especially relevant in forest areas where snake bites, animal bites, scorpion and bee stings are a regular phenomena.

o Early diagnosis of all severe illnesses

Apart from developing low-cost technologies for medical treatment, the JSS team, like Binayak and his health workers, trains and facilitates illiterate village women to provide health services for the community, well aware that doctors and nurses cannot reach every outpost that needs them.

~

"Very few doctors are going to rural India, hardly any people have started similar work after we have...it's a lonely world in rural health care," says Dr Yogesh Jain with a wry smile.

Made far more lonely and vulnerable when role models and mentors end up paying a heavy price for their work! The arrest and subsequent two-year incarceration of Binayak Sen for exposing human rights abuses in Bastar has led to considerable insecurity among the doctors at JSS, Ganyari.

Yogesh talks about how anxious they all were for his safety even before he was arrested. "A year before the arrest, we used to ask him why are you doing this, you won't be able to do all these things that you are doing, you will be picked up. And I remember him telling me, Yogesh, I can't stop doing this, there's no other way. And I would tell him how scared we all were for him."

Today as they hear allegations made by the state that despite being considered good doctors, they are also considered to be close to Binayak and therefore face allegations that they treat Naxalites, it is difficult for the JSS doctors not to feel similarly threatened. Being in the eye of the investigations, they face the very real fear of more state inquiries about their association with Binayak, and this could possibly jeopardize their work, but as Yogesh categorically puts it, they cannot stop the work they're doing and that's the other reason they consistently and openly supported Binayak and campaigned for his release.

It wasn't just because of their personal relationship with him, the fact that they are friends, have a history together. Yogesh has another, unique perspective on why Binayak was chosen as an index case to silence prospective voices of dissent. It was because he (Binayak) was a middle class doctor, like most of them, working in the field of inequity but coming from the middle class. Liking the good things of life, good food, music. Binayak is not someone who has declassed himself, he is not an outright, down and out activist. Had he been a totally political animal and *then* been picked up, the lesson would not have been so obvious. In his case, the right message was sent to the right quarters, according to Yogesh.

The Ganyari doctors were among the very few people in Chhattisgarh, especially among the medical fraternity, who were an active part of the Free Binayak Sen campaign. As friends, as activists and as people who provide the ideological underpinning to what public health is, they have been part of the process, the entire movement for justice. Yet, despite their sustained and fearless support of Binayak till he was released on bail, Yogesh feels a lot of damage has been done by his jail term since potential voices in Chhattisgarh and neighbouring states have effectively been silenced. Less people will be interested in moving to rural India due to Binayak being kept in jail for so long.

The sudden cries of a child interrupt our conversation and Yogesh invites a waiting couple with a sick child to come in, reassuring them that he will attend to them in ten minutes...yet another example of personalized attention at Ganyari and also my cue to wind up the interview.

I ask for any personal anecdote about Binayak and Yogesh obliges with a story about Binayak's beard! "We were travelling in a second class compartment in a train to Purulia some time in 1993, and someone came and asked Binayak, *'Maulanaji, kya time hua hai?'* That's when I asked him why he had grown a beard and he said he wanted to see what it means to be insecure, to know how it feels to be a minority in one's own country." With that parting statement Yogesh turns to his young patient and I decide to return to Anurag Bhargava's chambers.

~

The thronging crowd has dwindled somewhat but the stream of patients claiming Anurag's attention continues even as he gestures for me to step inside. The next hour passes by without my even realizing it, as successive patients enter the room with worried faces and walk out reassured and comforted.

His room is a sanctuary for the ill and needy, even though the trappings are exactly what one would expect in a small, low-cost clinic—an examining table, the doctor's desk and chair, two chairs on the opposite side, a stool on the right side.

Anurag Bhargava's academic credentials are no less impressive than Yogesh Jain's. Apart from the fact that both are founding members of JSS, Anurag too is a National Talent Search scholar with a post-graduate degree in Internal Medicine from AIIMS followed by a teaching stint there as well. Today he coordinates the medical services at JSS, as well as supervizes the functioning of one of the lowest cost pharmacies in India without any compromise on quality. As an active member of the All India Drug Action Network, Anurag engages regularly with the judiciary, executive, legislature, academia and lay people on the issue of a rational pharmaceutical policy and the urgent need for comprehensive price regulation in India.

In Yogesh's scale of good doctors, Anurag too would be termed a Type-2 plus doctor.

After the very last patient has left the room and I finally have his undivided attention, I ask the question that is predominant in my mind after observing the solicitous care given to rural patients by doctor after doctor at Ganyari. Are the JSS doctors inheritors of Binayak's legacy?

Anurag smiles deprecatingly and says that first, Binayak has not finished his work and second, everyone cannot be a Binayak. While Binayak's work is recognised as being overtly political, their combined struggle on various other important facets of public health continues—making health care more affordable, engaging with the government, with the bureaucracy, filing Public Interest Litigations or PILs, campaigning for price control. He and the other JSS doctors have worked hard to highlight such issues on a national level, despite seeing little success. Interestingly he tells me that for this kind of work, they get the support of the middle class, but for the kind of work Binayak does, there is no support, no allies, no understanding.

"Even doctors in general, for instance, cannot relate to Binayak. We had great difficulty in explaining the case to them, since any kind of social role for doctors is not inculcated and any training given in social and preventive medicine is superficial. In any case, very few doctors enter that sphere. Binayak continues to be one of the rare ones. In my view, it's a complete failure of the whole system of medical education which is just producing technicians who are interested in making money. If Binayak was in Latin America, he would be completely recognizable and people would respond to him because that whole model of health care is based on a social and political understanding of their needs. Rudolph Virchow puts it aptly when he says that health is politics and politics is nothing but medicine on a grand scale," says Anurag emphatically.

Health is a human right, health is a product of social determinance. Ultimately it is political...access to health, access to a road, in the end, it's all political, says Anurag. *This* is how Binayak treated health care. Not just by knowing people by their names but by helping development through education, through agriculture, through providing legal aid when needed, guiding people through a very different dimension from an ordinary doctor operating in rural India. Walking the alternative route towards medicine, doing "low tech" capacity building work, teaching and training health workers to be responsive, available, sensitive to community needs. None of this is glamorous work, nobody gets a Padma Bhushan for it, the only reward being the undying gratitude of scores of poor people who have no one else to turn to. People whose entire savings of a lifetime can get erased by a single episode of hospitalization. People who walk 30-40 kilometres on empty stomachs to reach a government health centre where more often than not, there is no doctor to attend to their problems, to treat their sickness, to just listen to what they have to say about their pain.

Just one example of the extreme odds that need to be overcome in the struggle to access health care is illustrated in a newspaper article by Sujeet Kumar about 25-year old Phoolwati who walked a record 110 kilometres for fifteen days to reach a government-run hospital to get her burnt hands treated. The kerosene stove in her hut in Bakalo village of Raigarh district in Chhattisgarh burst without warning and in the absence of medical treatment, Phoolwati's husband Roop Singh battled his burn injuries for a week and then died. When Phoolwati found insects crawling inside her burnt hands, she decided to get treatment but since she had absolutely no money for either consulting a private doctor or taking a bus to the government hospital in Raigarh, she walked the entire distance, begging for food from local people along the road. The doctor who cleaned her wound that was filled with insects said that she would have definitely lost both her hands had she come in for treatment even a week later. These are the people nobody even knows about, much less care about their deprivation and suffering.

Binayak Sen was one of the rare breed of doctors—like the Ganyari staff—who cared about the marginalized, the disadvantaged, the forgotten.

Naturally enough, being so intricately involved in this process, when he often saw ill health as an outcome of hunger, the kind of agricultural technology being foisted on people and so on, he responded to those issues. Thus his work acquired "political" overtones when in fact what he was doing was looking at health the way it should be addressed. Raising a very clear and consistent voice and stand against human rights abuses, he was one of the first to venture into the disturbed areas and express concern. That took great moral courage, especially as Binayak was the first to honestly admit to both Yogesh and Anurag that while he did feel afraid of the consequences, he just had to keep on doing what he had to do, he had no choice in the matter.

Anurag freely admits to Binayak being their mentor, someone whose advice and guidance has been consistent for the JSS doctors, and even though he doesn't play a day-to-day role in the functioning of the organization, he remains one of the people whose association with public health in rural areas has been long and sustained and therefore worthy of emulation. The JSS health care programme incorporates many of Binayak's values. Indeed it owes its very existence, in part, to the fact that Binayak was an important figure in primary health care in the state, a factor that was considered when the AIIMS doctors were scouting for areas to operate in.

Despite their vigorous assertions that they are not, and cannot be, future Binayaks, the similarities and synergies between the Ganyari doctors and their mentor are clearly there to see, especially in any discussions about carrying forward a legacy of dedicated service to the rural poor. As highly trained professionals who had more lucrative and socially acceptable options available in multi-speciality hospitals anywhere in the country or the world, the Ganyari doctors, like Binayak before them, chose to set up base in a remote area that others had ignored. And while they might not be overtly "political" today, their own classification of being Type 2 (plus) doctors could well change over time to the admired Type 3 doctor that Binayak is seen by them to be, given the fact that there is an age difference of perhaps fifteen-odd years between them.

No less a person than Ilina Sen validates the torch being passed on to the JSS doctors, simultaneoulsy reiterating that Binayak has many years' work left in him. "JSS is a critical medical facility and while it may not have the political and human rights dimension that led Binayak or Rupantar or Shaheed to work towards handing over control to the people, nevertheless, in a lot of ways, JSS is taking it beyond Binayak," she says firmly.

Binayak was among the first people to work in the 'falciparum' malaria endemic regions in Chhattisgarh but the structure that he built up was not able to handle all the issues. She explains, "JSS was able to raise serious questions about the state government-sponsored treatment regime in a recent national consultation on malaria, taking forward the health agenda for rural areas which

Binayak was perhaps not able to do as much."

Yogesh provides details about the two day workshop on 'falciparum' malaria control held at JSS, Ganyari in February 2009. The recommendations that followed the discussions led to a new programme being launched in Chhattisgarh.

Binayak continues to be their mentor, continues to talk to them, they continue to be close even though it was difficult for them as they were targeted for being close to him, says Ilina.

Most importantly, like Binayak, the Ganyari doctors do not see their choice as a "sacrifice".

~

In the unhurried pace of the daily schedule at JSS, as I wait impatiently for the doctors who offered me a lift back to Bilaspur in their jeeps (my autorickshaw having been long dismissed) I realize I am the only one around here whose time is self-centred.

An hour goes by. The explanation for the delay is simple. Anurag is waiting for some blood reports of a patient even as the rest of us, two jeep-loads of people (six or seven doctors and I), wait for him. He finally arrives, unapologetic but smiling, and we set off on the return journey.

The setting sun adds to the beauty of the scenic ride, the smile on my face has only become wider, combined as it is with the warm glow in my heart at having met people with substance, with ideals, with compassion, in a world fast losing touch with such emotions and aspirations.

By the time I reach Bilaspur railway station it is way past 7 pm and I have missed my train to Raipur.

My only wish however, as I sit eating a cold masala dosa at the platform's tiny restaurant, is for the same day to start all over again.

Chapter Six

FAMILY TIES

Raipur and Mumbai

The first time I saw Pranhita, the feisty twenty-five-year-old elder daughter of Binayak and Ilina Sen, she was quietly and unobtrusively taking photographs on her Nikon camera. It was the evening of May 13, 2009, an evening of cultural performances to express solidarity with Binayak Sen who was at that time in Raipur Central Jail. The venue was a small stadium in Raipur and the function was aptly titled *Mukti Utsav,* held in support of the Free Binayak Sen campaign.

As people from diverse groups and regions trooped in, and as performer followed performer for the next five hours, Pranhita continued to record images of people gathered together to protest against her father's continued imprisonment. Singers, dancers, poets, film makers and activists took their turn onstage, keeping a 350-odd audience spellbound with their expressions of protest, of outrage, of freedom.

No one took a tea or even a water break.

Pranhita watched and took pictures, sitting alone, even though her mother Ilina was also present, applauding the artistes. Earlier in the evening as we all waited together for the stadium to fill up, watching groups of people trickle in, Pranhita had told me she wanted to pursue a career in cinematography.

The next day, the second anniversary of the day her father was jailed, Pranhita was clicking pictures again, first seated on the floor at the partially-covered, dusty Budha Talab venue, as various speeches were delivered by activists, lawyers, doctors, trade unionists, students' unions, demanding unconditional bail for Binayak.

Later, in the scorching afternoon heat, *dupatta* wrapped around her head for protection, she walked, one with the 600-strong crowd of her father's supporters, shouting slogans as loudly as the others, but also recording the march towards Central Jail on her trusted Nikon.

As I walked along with her for the 3 kilometres stretch, wincing at the hot road under my inadequate shoes, she smiled in sympathy, offering her bottle of water to me. Almost two hours later, even as the police clamped Section 144 to halt the procession, an effigy of the Salwa Judum and the Chhattisgarh Special Protection of Securities Act or CSPSA was burnt outside Subhash Stadium which then doubled up as a temporary jail, with 250 supporters courting arrest in a peaceful sit-in with Budhan Bai's voice singing, "We don't want your blows and bullets, we don't want your unfair laws and government, we want freedom...*aazadi de hammanla.*"

Despite the presence of both the media and the police, Pranhita continued to search for the best angles to take her photographs, protected by her relative anonymity, raising her voice just once when a photographer came in close to click her, "No pictures please," she told him firmly and he retreated hurriedly.

Since I was filming the event too, I asked her some impromptu questions at the stadium while we waited for the symbolic arrests to be completed. What kind of man commands support like this, from people who may never even have met him? What part of the Binayak Sen story touches people's hearts enough to make them travel long distances and walk in the 43 degree afternoon heat to fight for his freedom?

She hesitated, laughing nervously, begging me to ask a simpler question so I switched to her father's arrest. And her indignation spilled out immediately. "I would like to say that the way the state government is portraying my father...he's not a Maoist, he's not a terrorist, he's a very simple man who loves people, who likes to interact with people. He wants to work among the poor people and help them with their problems. I think whatever my father did was the correct thing and I will always support him," she said emphatically.

I quizzed her about an interview published in a Mumbai daily about her wanting to make a film on her father's life. She admitted she wanted to, some day, and we left it at that, leaving the stadium that was located right next to the jail that housed Binayak.

The next time I saw Pranhita was on television, eleven days later, hugging her father outside that same jail in Raipur, both of them wearing beaming smiles.

Her father had been released on bail.

~

Two months later I finally get a chance to talk to her at length about her father being her hero, about her "different" childhood and her own experiences during his jail term. We are in the CMC Vellore campus where the family is camped for the duration of Ilina's chemotherapy treatment.

Pranhita wears mostly salwar-kameez, her be-spectacled serious look belying her spirited nature, her infectious laugh. Her most striking characteristic is a fearless attitude towards whatever life has in store for her. She makes a dismissive gesture with her hands, "I think I'm very different from others, a little *hatke*. Initially I may have less confidence but if I feel I can do something then no one can stop me."

I wonder whether her matter-of-fact tone, her air of youthful bravado in describing threats she faced not so long ago are a cover-up for the very real fear she must have experienced. "When Baba was in jail and Ma was in Wardha (Ilina is the head of the Department of Women's Studies at the Mahatma Gandhi Institute, Wardha) I was staying alone in the Raipur flat and commuting to my university in Khairagarh daily. After a month, I started getting leaflets, written on them in big, bold letters, 'We know you live alone, we have seen you in court, we know you commute alone every day, we know your bus route, we know the number of hours you spend there, we will kill you.' Baba was in jail and they wanted to scare me, so what? Let anyone touch me, I will deal with them. *Koi chhu ke bata de, maar denge!*" she declares with a flourish.

I like her spirit and say so.

The fear was and continues to be for her father, not for her own personal safety, she says. She tells me of a recent argument with Binayak about not wanting him to go back there (the Salwa Judum dominated areas in Bastar). She was scared they might kill him.

A normal, middle class family leading a normal, middle class life, now facing fears that no one else who has not walked a similar path can begin to imagine! Only it really wasn't a normal, middle class life, Pranhita corrects me, talking of her unconventional upbringing and "free" childhood.

She was always aware that her parents were different, Baba and Ma, she tells me laughingly. All kinds of people would come to the Sen home, poor, rich, elite, tribals, intellectuals. Discussions would go on late into the night, the talking appeared endless. The initial feeling of her space being invaded, of people sleeping on their beds, later changed to acceptance and awareness once she grew up, understood the issues, saw the work they did. Even today though, she admits that sometimes she wonders about it all... "*pata nahin kya hai yeh.*"

Growing up different meant her friends too made her feel different, asking her who all the people who trooped in and out of her home were, why they were there, questions she couldn't answer at that point since she didn't really know or understand what her parents did, she only knew bits and pieces of their life. She put it together much later when she voluntarily accompanied her parents on their PUCL investigations.

Her first exposure (as a young, thinking adult) to her parents' life with its attendant struggle and danger was the Golapalli investigation in 2004. Two students and a teacher lost their lives while another teacher was badly injured and taken to Bhadrachalam. Pranhita, who was doing the videography for PUCL for this investigation, went to Bhadrachalam to interview the sole survivor eyewitness and thus got a first-hand feel of the situation.

She admits to a fascination, a love for Bastar that draws her again and again to the place and its people. "Every time anyone goes to Bastar, I tell them I want to go too. Even when Baba had gone for the Salwa Judum investigations in 2005, I went with him. The place is so beautiful, the people are so friendly, they seem like your own people that you need to help," she says.

I ask her if it's the hidden journalist in her (given that she has just completed her Mass Communication course from Xaviers College, Mumbai) that prompted her to go for the investigations and she laughs and says she's no journalist! She's a good listener though, she tells me, and when she went to Golapalli it was very clear to her what it was all about. Her father's earlier investigations into land acquisitions in Bastar, and subsequent harassment by goons on his return, had alarmed her.

Not any more. Pranhita displays rare courage and fortitude in dealing with an uncertain future, with her father's trial still not over and standing rock-like alongside her mother for the entire duration of her medical treatment.

I am curious to know more about her childhood and prod her into recalling her earliest memories of doing things with her father. "Baba was one of my earliest teachers of maths and he was a good teacher but he used to beat me sometimes." She laughs uproariously at my shocked expression. The gentle, soft-spoken Binayak Sen I have interacted with, an impression that countless other people have corroborated, does not coincide with the image of him beating his daughter over a maths lesson. It is a revelation but Pranhita is unconcerned, merely informing me that he tried hard to teach her maths and that she was a total zero in the subject.

She also remembers magical moments of living in a forest, sitting in front of a fire at night, chatting away and watching the stars in the sky, something one rarely sees in cities. "Baba, Ma and I would look at the constellation, Baba would tell me that one is Orion, that is Big Bear. It was so much fun, that whole atmosphere, that whole way of life was fantastic," she says fondly.

Photographs of baby Pranhita strapped onto a harness on Binayak's back while he cycles to work are part of a collection I have seen at the Niyogi household too, as also pictures of Jeet Niyogi and Pranhita playing together with chickens...but of course she was too young to remember those days.

"Today Binayak Sen is a hero for many people..." I start and she interrupts me mid-sentence to say laughingly, "For me also. He has always been a hero, and now he's more of a hero to me than even before! His best quality I think is that he listens to you, he doesn't talk much but he thinks a lot, he listens and then he'll give you an answer or tell you whatever he is thinking. He's very down-to-earth, very polite, almost saintly...sometimes we call him Saint Binayak." Her hearty laughter mixes with mine.

Is Binayak a hands-on father in terms of her career goals? Is he clued into her future plans? He tries to be, she says truthfully; when he was in jail, he tried to be involved in whatever both children were doing but it was limited. Once he got out, the participation was much more. Discussions on whether she should go in for editing or cinematography, watching films together, chatting about them, are now routine. The entire family, both her parents have become very interested in cinema since her decision to work with film, she says proudly. "We watch trailers and promos of films on TV and after watching the first scene, I'll tell the name of the film and he'll say 'How do you know all these things?'"

~

Much later, in Mumbai, I get a chance to meet Aparajita, or Billo who is completing her graduation in History from Sophia College.

Dressed in a bright green kurta over classic blue jeans, she rushes out of class, apologizing for being ten minutes late and we drive to a restaurant she suggests for lunch. "We come here every Sunday for dinner as a treat," she shares. Sitting across a table from her, I notice her pretty eyes. They change colour with whatever she wears, she says shyly in response to my compliment.

Today they are greenish brown and glow brighter when she is animated.

Aparajita Sen is an unusual nineteen-year-old, wise beyond her years, one who has learnt how to handle the punches life doles out. On account of all that has happened to her father and family, she has had to grow up fast. "You can't hope for things to be all right," she says, "you have to fight to make them all right. Expecting any fair play from these people is absurd, you have to be ready for the worst…seeing all these things, I grew up quickly. Somewhere I feel I didn't have a chance to find my feet in my own world," she says matter-of-factly.

She was in the 10th standard when her father was arrested and she could not accept why only he was targeted or why others in PUCL who did what he did were not in jail. Why did they pick on Binayak alone? Then, when she saw the number of supporters for her father's release, she felt a little more reassured.

Meetings with Binayak in jail were most inadequate and left her feeling angry and helpless. "We could not touch him, hug him, there was a net and then bars behind it. Everything we would send him, small things like vegetables, tomatoes etc. they (jail authorities) would check it. Once outside court (when the trial was on), while he was waiting in the van, he passed me his copy of the chargesheet to hold and when I was passing it back to him later, one official said I could not do that because I may be adding something to it and giving it to Baba!" she says indignantly. Whenever she thinks or talks about these things she is filled with frustration, she tells me. "Baba lost his entire independence, the only independence he had left was that he could breathe on his own."

She talks of her mother with simple pride. "She is the backbone of the family. She never let us feel alone, she inspired us to do our daily routine work. She put in a lot of effort to keep us smiling. Once I attended a party with my friends and someone made a snide comment about me partying while my father was in jail and Ma said Baba being in jail doesn't mean I should stop living my life!"

Billo also had to make a crucial decision about her studies while her father was in jail. Without the benefit of his advice, she had to choose whether she wanted to pursue science or arts. Having chosen science in the 11th standard against her real inclination, she realized her mistake when she got 57 per cent and saw her friends struggling with tuitions for the 11th, 12th and medical entrance exams simultaneously. So she opted for Arts in Sophia College in Mumbai and wants to study law later and fight injustice, like her father. "Science was just not my cup of tea. I know my father wanted me to become a doctor but I also saw the way the system worked, how the villagers had to wait for such a long time, how nobody bothered about anyone else's pain and it made me angry," says Billo.

She is lucky to have parents who never pressurized her to get high marks or got disappointed when she didn't, she informs me. Binayak may have wanted her to follow in his footsteps and pursue medicine but when he saw she was uncomfortable with doing Science, he supported her decision to take up Arts. "When my 12th standard results came out and I got 61 per cent, I thought that was very bad and started crying on the phone to Ma who asked me if I had failed! Then she told me it doesn't matter, you did whatever you could have done. Baba said we love you for who you are."

Billo too has stories about Binayak the impatient maths teacher! "Baba taught me maths and science till the 10th standard though I had tuitions too. He was not a good teacher, very impatient. I used to be horrified when I saw him beat Didi, though he never used to beat me. My maths was a bit better than Didi's but still I would insist on Ma being present in the house when Baba taught me maths!" she says laughingly. "But he was not a strict father," she hastens to clarify, "he never hassled me about marks though he did insist on exams being a time to 'revise, not study'. Once I hadn't done an entire chapter in maths just the day before the exam and went to ask him at 10 pm. He asked me what is it you don't understand and I had to confess I didn't understand the whole chapter and he lost it!"

Ilina was a much better teacher, relaxed, veering from history, geography to talk about friends, just about any topic. "*Gappe zyada, padhai kam hoti thi.* But they were the best parents ever!" she declares happily. They may have been different from the parents of her friends but today, she considers herself lucky when she compares her childhood with that of her friends. She was exposed to a more real world, to a life that extended beyond one's own little domain, one's own town or city, one's own problems. And this was done gradually so she could absorb it step by step. "My parents would take me to Bhilai for Niyogiji's *shraddhanjali* each year so I would get to know about the CMM and Niyogiji and things like that. They would tell me why they were doing certain types of work, they would explain this is what happens...and I learnt about life on a large scale," says Billo earnestly.

Though Billo, unlike Pranhita, never lived in small places like Dalli Rajhara, she remembers visits to Bagrumnala and other villages, she tells me how she made friends with a tribal girl called Meena with whom she would go into the forest and pick tendu leaves and help make bundles. Taking a bath in the pond was another unique experience. "My friends in Raipur could never relate to these experiences when I would talk about a bath in an open pond, no proper bathrooms, life without electricity. After a while I stopped trying to tell them. They were used to thinking only about themselves. They never knew about my parents' work," she says without rancour.

She herself understood the real nature of her father's work for the first time when he went to Nagarnar in 2002 on the Orissa-Chhattisgarh border on an investigation and the entire house was filled with tension till he returned. Her parents' earlier work at Bagrumnala and with the women's groups had not caused the disturbance that Binayak's investigations subsequently did, even though she was still too young, ten or eleven, to know too much about it at the time. Today she is proud of her father for doing something that was really hard to do, for paving the route for people to see that another world exists, a world that needs help.

Her voice turns wistful as she adds, "What I really want is to see Baba and Ma more relaxed. From childhood I have seen them working 24×7, both of them never got the chance to ever do the little, little things they wanted to do. I would like to picture them reading books in a room with dogs around, music on, Ma drinking *chai* in a large mug."

I ask her if she is scared of Binayak pursuing his crusade against the Salwa Judum. Yes, she fears for his life but deals with the fear by determinedly pushing it away. "As long as the four of us are together, I will never feel insecure, as long as the family is with me. All of us love to travel, that's how we would ideally like to unwind, by travelling, chatting, with *chai* breaks," she smiles.

Her personal wish-list is, by her own admission, endless. She wants to do everything...theatre (she was at a month-long NSD workshop in Delhi when Binayak was released on bail and took two days leave to join the family in Raipur), trekking, play the violin, badminton, an internship with the PUCL...she is Binayak Sen's daughter after all! Not surprisingly, her mother is a role model too. "My friends' mothers were all housewives and Ma was not but that was fine. I feel every woman should work and be self-reliant. I can adjust to any situation because of the way Ma-Baba brought me up," she ends confidently.

~

The underlying strength and resilience that one observes in both the daughters of Binayak and Ilina Sen, in their coping with unforeseen, harsh circumstances with fortitude, is testimony to the way they have been brought up.

Ilina talks about how difficult it must have been for her daughters, especially Billo, to accept that both their parents were not cast in the so-called "normal" parent mould. Ilina was not the perfect housewife-mother who cooked for her children. Binayak was not the father with a steady job and a steady income. Understanding this, internalizing it, respecting their parents for what and who they were, confronting peer group pressure to conform, was tough and Ilina is justifiably proud that they were able to stand together through it all, through the ordeal of imprisonment and uncertainty thereafter.

When you look at Ilina Sen initially, you only notice the serene face and gentle smile that matches an equally gentle voice. After a very short period however, you realize the sheer range and capability with which she takes on and completes the many, *many* tasks in the Sen household. Any question about Binayak's schedule, the family's travel plans, Pranhita's career options, availability of information about PUCL files or Salwa Judum atrocities, contact numbers for health workers at the Bagrumnala clinic, issues related to the Free Binayak Sen campaign, are all efficiently addressed by her.

When I comment on her seemingly endless reserves of strength she smiles wryly. "When you are thrust into a situation, you have no choice but to cope." But that is an obvious understatement and does not begin to describe the reality she lived through in the two years of her husband's imprisonment, his subsequent heart ailment diagnosis followed soon after by her own surgery and treatment for breast cancer. By unspoken mutual consent both of us consciously avoid the topic of her illness though there are times when you cannot help but notice her pain, reflected visibly on her mobile face and often, even in her voice over the telephone.

Ilina rarely talks about her own trials and tribulations.

At the May 13, 2009 *Mukti Utsav* in Raipur, she had told me on videotape that the fact that Binayak was still alive and had not been physically harmed, that the family had somehow managed to carry on was entirely due to the media attention given to the case and the support of so many people.

A few months later, at CMC Vellore, with her husband sitting reassuringly nearby, she describes the unbearable loneliness she underwent when Binayak was in jail. "I did go through some very bad times, times of great loneliness but at the same time, overall there was this feeling that I am not alone. I had so many people staying with me throughout, either Kavita Srivastava, PUCL activist-lawyer or Sudha Bhardwaj, trade unionist-lawyer or someone else. I would come back to Raipur over the weekend and usually there would be someone there. Yet there were times when I felt weepy. When Pranhita and Billo had gone to Mumbai, I would return on Friday night or early Saturday morning to this empty house and step inside to encounter this old lizard in the kitchen, living under my oven. Finally the only sign of life in the house was this lizard and I would come and look for it, this familiar lizard would make me feel things are okay," she laughs deprecatingly.

Ilina has many answers to my oft-repeated question about why so many people supported her and Binayak. First, both Binayak and she were people who had worked in the development sector with the progressive intelligentsia of the country for many years, so there was a large network to which they were already connected. Then, Binayak's alma mater CMC Vellore stepped in almost immediately. "CMC really protects and nurtures its own. I had witnessed that when I was here earlier. Even then so many people had become friends, but the way they all came together was a revelation for me...the CMC alumni, the CMC college staff, the students, professors. Also, for many people who realized that the state and system are rotten, Salwa Judum had already become something to be talked about. Nandigram and Singrur also happened at roughly the same time, so many people were moved by the issue of land acquisition, issue of state violence. Many people in different parts of the country at that particular time had begun to understand, make the inter-connections and this case brought the outrage out into the open. People were able to relate to this. Binayak's case epitomized everything that was wrong. *That's* what brought people together across politics, across different spectrums," she analyses.

She curses herself for not realizing what she had been witness to in her childhood years, growing up in the North-East, what the people of the North-East had gone through for sixty years, till she connected with the same issues when Chhattisgarh became such a violent place to live in. The resonances were always there, she says ruefully and then tells me about the North-East years as well as about the years that went before.

Ilina was born in the early fifties and courtesy an army background (like Binayak's), her earliest memories are of growing up in various places—in Kashmir, in Delhi, travelling to Kolkata each year for long vacations with a large extended family of aunts and uncles she was close to, many of whom had bitter experiences during the Partition of East Bengal, their home. This explains why the entire issue of displacement and migration is of such interest to her and why both she and Binayak (whose family roots also go back to East Bengal) can relate to it. It explains (perhaps) the choice of Demography as her PhD subject from Jawaharlal Nehru University (JNU), Delhi. She also did a Post-Doctoral work in France on historical demography. But it is the North-East experience that she considers unique, influencing her unconsciously till conscious awareness kicked in years later in Chhattisgarh.

Ilina attended school in Shillong, Meghalaya. When she was in the 11th standard, one of her classmates, a Mizo, failed to turn up after the winter vacation. She re-appeared only in June. It was the year of the Mizo uprising and the Mizo National Front had tracked down and shot dead her father and brother-in-law. The girl, along with her mother and older sister, trekked a distance of 200 kilometres to Silchar and from there, made it to Shillong so she could re-join school. This incident along with its ramifications had an impact on Ilina only in the years to come. What also lay dormant within her, to surface much later, were the stories of suffering, displacement, the role of the state in conflict areas, nationality issues raised by her Mizo fellow students. Somewhere deep inside her, these issues remained.

It was after acquiring her college degree from Kolkata that Ilina got married to Binayak. I ask her what attracted her to him at the age of twenty. "Puppy love," she smiles in memory. "Our mothers went to the same school so the families knew each other, were friends. But we became close only in Binayak's final year of medical college, when he visited us at Jabalpur." Reminiscences of "starry-eyed days a long time ago" bring a faraway look to Ilina's face.

Binayak on the other hand, refuses to talk about this part of his life. I mention to him that many people think of them as an ideal couple but "I am not going to discuss this kind of thing," he says, his tone dismissive and abrupt. When I persist, tell him about the number of his colleagues and friends who have expressed how much of a role Ilina has played in his life and work through her support, he gets almost annoyed. "There's no question of her support. Whatever we do, we do together. And it's not just Ilina and I, there are so many others working with us, like us, and I am very proud of that...singling Ilina and me is not fair and it's not justified," he asserts.

When I put the same question to Ilina, fortunately for me, she answers with a smile and in some detail. Love has many stages, she says meditatively. Initially it was puppy love, Binayak was very good looking, he was gentle, with an attractive personality, he spoke well and the two of them had a lot of common interests. "I don't know about ideal couple but both of us have struggled to stay with each other, emotionally, intellectually. After so many years of marriage—thirty seven—we respect each other, so in that sense it has been a very unique partnership."

Staying with each other also meant sharing issues that were important to both of them. Ilina cites examples which range from simple family concerns to larger issues. For instance, she grew up in an animal-loving family, with an animal rights activist mother, and five or six dogs in her home at any given point. Binayak came from a family that did not allow dogs inside a house. But he adapted and today their farm in Bhatagaon on the outskirts of Raipur is inhabited by seven dogs! Binayak also took the trouble to educate himself on subjects that interested her such as gender studies, sociology, development. In turn, she tried to relate to the issues closest to him, partnering Binayak in his overall trajectory at each and every stage and that according to her is the secret of the "ideal couple" tag bestowed on them by those who have witnessed their bond over the years.

~

Of the many admirers of the Ilina-Binayak *jodi* is Binayak's youngest brother Deepankar. He is vocal about his opinion. "Ilina and Dada are an exceptional, made-for-each-other couple. The way in which she has handled this entire crisis, commuting from Wardha to Raipur, doing her teaching job, finding accommodation for her daughters, coping with all the prison formalities, the lawyers, the bail petitions, it's just amazing," he says emphatically.

I meet Deepankar Sen first for a formal interview in Mumbai and then informally outside the corridors of the fast-track court in Raipur, waiting along with Binayak for the judge to begin proceedings. And then again, over an extended lunch at the Sen home at Surya apartments that same afternoon.

The physical resemblance between Binayak and Deepankar is undeniable—the same sharp features, the same quick, disarming smile, the physicality in terms of height (though Binayak is more frail now), even their voices that sound quite alike. But the similarities end there and Deepankar is the first one to openly say so. "Our paths were diametrically opposite. I couldn't wait to go off abroad. In fact, I have lived abroad from 1979 onwards. I led a five-star life, far *far* remote from Dada's. I never had a clue about his kind of life, the clinics he ran in places I had never heard of like Dalli Rajhara!" he says with disarming candour.

Having studied Spanish at JNU, he wanted to become an interpreter at the UN but joined Sita World to promote tourism from Spain, Portugal and Latin America. This world of glamour which he thoroughly enjoyed was followed by a stint in the oil industry in Switzerland for seven years, with him ultimately ending up in Belgium, in commodities trading, his current profession in India. His only aim was to make money, to have more and more, "a self-generating process of greed and accumulation." When he did visit his brother in Raipur he would stay at Babylon Inn, the city's best hotel instead of the two-bedroom flat in Surya apartments.

For long years while Deepankar was living his capitalist world abroad and Binayak his own special one in rural India (which Deepankar didn't understand), there was a huge gap between the brothers, says Deepankar, but the arrest and subsequent struggle changed all that. He was in Paris when Pranhita called to inform him about Binayak being in jail and he was astounded and angry and continues to be frustrated that something like this can happen to a good, gentle person like his brother. He came to stand by his brother during the trying two-year period and this time, he stayed at their home. He saw first-hand the range of support his brother garnered, from poor tribal villagers to activists to intellectuals and it helped him understand Binayak better.

Watching Deepankar hover protectively around Binayak, trying to anticipate his needs, helping take care in whatever manner he can, one can see the attempt at change that he openly talks about. "I still don't fully understand the world that drives Dada, it is genuine care for people, and it is very difficult to get involved without having those qualities but more than anything else, he's my brother, it's my responsibility to look after him just like he's looked after me all my life." He feels that Binayak is perhaps the only person after Gandhi who has caught the imagination of so many who supported him because of his genuine concern for people. He feels privileged today to have been born into the same family.

Deepankar may appear to have rediscovered his older brother today but he also tells me Binayak was always his hero because he always looked out for him. "Right from school, each time I had a problem I would write to him. Then later on, living in Switzerland, living in Belgium, if I had a headache I would call across continents to ask his advice first. He would rarely give it, he would say go see a doctor, but just to know that I had spoken to him would calm me down. In the two years that he was in jail what I missed the most was talking to him, about *my* problems, it was always me talking about my problems. He's like a sponge, he has the capacity to absorb everyone's problems, and a gentleness, a calmness I have not seen in anyone else so far." He adds a simple statement that comes from the heart. "He's not just a brother, he's someone who's very nice to have around."

As someone who was physically beside his brother when he was released on bail and witnessed Binayak's commitment to continue his campaign against the Salwa Judum and to fight for human rights, is Deepankar worried about the future? His answer is characteristically frank. "Dada is so fearless because he is driven by the courage of his convictions, he doesn't fear for his life, he has his own agenda and he knows it will be long and rough and amazingly, he's not scared! If it does me or him any good to worry, I will be very worried but it won't. So I would rather join him in his path, support him in any way I can rather than worry."

He tells me about his mother crying during Binayak's jail term, asking him, "Will I live to see my son free?" Deepanker would tell her she didn't have permission to give up, to die just yet, she had to carry on.

Anusuya Sen was eighty-one when she wrote an impassioned letter in Bengali pleading for justice for her imprisoned son:

> "Should I regard as justice the refusal of bail to one who even as a child was moved by injustice, who having devoted his entire working life selflessly to providing food and health to the poor, who without coveting wealth, survived for days on dal, rice and green chillies, who is accustomed to living like the poor, and who is now arraigned for breach of public security and waging war against the state? If this is justice, where should I seek redress against injustice? Is justice so elusive in our free, democratic country?"

Her second son, Gautam Sen translated this letter into English and it was published in the Bangla edition of "The Statesman". "My mother is a very strong lady, only close family members ever see any hint of weakness," says Gautam. He is the middle brother who has been teaching in a private school in Istanbul since 1997. On a family vacation in Kalyani at the Sen home, Gautam talks of how rare it is for all three brothers to be together with their mother and that perhaps the last time he can recall such an occasion was when their father was alive.

Since the conversation is over the telephone, some threads are lost and some are scattered, and I string them together much like Gautam is doing with childhood stories of the three of them criss-crossing lives, criss-crossing cities, criss-crossing ambitions. The three Sen boys, separated in age by three to four years each, (and Gautam and Binayak by even less) studying together for a while and then going their separate ways, overlapping years and holidays, finally each one walking alone.

Gautam tries piecing the years together. "I remember long road trips in a Hillman car, a cross-country Delhi to Mumbai journey, I think that was. Earlier, from 1955-58, Dad (Colonel Deva Prasad Sen) was posted in Delhi, then Mumbai, where we lived on Cadell Road, then he got a field posting and we all moved to Calcutta. The infamous Calcutta Boys School or CBS, where Dada and I overlapped for a bit. I was in Class 8 when he completed his Senior Cambridge."

Gautam and Binayak share the most horrific memories of CBS, most especially of its principal C Hicks, who was nicknamed 'Chicks', chuckles Gautam over the phone, the glee apparent in his voice even decades later. Apparently Mr Hicks had a penchant for thrashing boys and Gautam was at the receiving end too. "Dada asked me once why I stood by and took it," he recalls.

Binayak at sixty can still shudder talking about his CBS days and the principal's treatment of him that was his own particular cross to bear at the young age of thirteen or fourteen. Each day would bring uncertainty for the young Binayak since Mr Hicks had an extreme love-hate relationship with him. "I was very good in my studies, which is not at all something that makes me very happy or proud, it just separated me from all my friends, so in the days he was pleased with me, he would hold me up as some kind of a genius. On days he was displeased with me, he would hold me up as a monster-figure, criticizing me for defects in character. I was very absent-minded. Once I'd start reading a book I would lose track of whatever was around. We were supposed to do certain tasks and if I was reading a book, sometimes I would forget to do these tasks. My forgetfulness was held up as an example of how I considered myself too superior to others," says Binayak wonderingly. Incredibly enough, even as an adult, Binayak has been told that he wakes up shouting about his experiences at that school, that in his sleep he mutters about the principal!

Moving past horror stories of Chicks, Gautam remembers Binayak writing wonderful short stories in a remarkably neat handwriting that has not changed over the years. His earliest memory of his brother is a summer holiday in Lucknow in 1962. They were both returning to the dreaded CBS with their mother feeling sorry for them. Gautam at age ten or eleven was crying away and Binayak was trying to comfort him.

He condenses the next few years for me. He speaks of his father's teaching year in Pune, with the rest of the family going to Jabalpur. Binayak left for college and then Vellore and from then on, says Gautam, one saw less and less of him. Gautam himself finished school in December 1967 then went on to St Stephen's in Delhi where he completed his post-graduation. For a while he taught economics and history at Rishi Valley and the Kodaikanal International School before finally moving to Turkey where he resides today.

By his own admission, his life, like Deepankar's, is drastically different from Binayak's. "I've made brief visits to Dada's clinics, seen his work, discovered areas of darkness in myself. But the way Dada and Ilina straddle two worlds, the urban middle class and the tribal world, is something I could never aspire to, I am too cloistered in my existence," he states. And yet, since 2004, Gautam runs a blog, "Gyanoprobha", featuring topics related to history, politics, development, gender, environment and human rights. During his brother's jail term, the blog focused almost exclusively on various aspects of the Binayak Sen story. Today "Gyanoprobha" explores many more issues.

I ask him if he too is closer to his brother after this ordeal, the way Deepankar has admitted to being, and Gautam agrees. "I'm closer to Dada now, more aware of what he's doing. Earlier there were long gaps between meetings, everyone led their own lives. Now we keep track of each other. My relationship with Dada is altered. Before this we never used to talk about politics, peace agendas...it's very important not to be cynical. People are trying to muddy the waters, trashing my brother's work. It distresses me that Dada is not clued into the often nasty side of the public, the internet jackals, the laptop owning class, even at times, a manipulative media."

Ending on a rueful note, he remarks that it shouldn't have taken his brother being in jail for two years for the family to come together. The reunion at Kalyani seems hard won in more ways than one.

Chapter Seven

THE TURNING POINT: SALWA JUDUM

Dantewada

Salwa Judum, original meaning: Purification Hunt, also Peace March, in the tribal Gondi language. Designated as an anti- Naxalite movement which began in Chhattisgarh in April 2005, supported by both the BJP and the Congress, the two largest political parties in India, it is also claimed to be a "spontaneous uprising" of local people against the Naxalites. It is more commonly described as a state-sponsored counter insurgency operation that has involved vigilante gangs accompanied by state security forces called the Special Police Officers, or SPOs, who have burned villages, killed tribals and forced them into camps, all as part of the effort to counter the Naxalites or Maoists. Over 644 villages have been cleared or evacuated and more than 3 lakh tribals displaced.

He may deny it, and he may not like it, but forty-five-year-old Himanshu Kumar, mild-mannered, white kurta pyjama-clad, is the new poster boy for human rights activism in the country today. He has been living in the state of Chhattisgarh for the last seventeen years. More specifically, in faraway, godforsaken Dantewada, two and a half hours from Jagdalpur, Bastar. Home to the poorest of tribals, home to Himanshu, until the government demolished his ashram and later drove him out of his temporary shelter as well, punishing him for going beyond the acceptable limit of the developmental work that he had been doing for almost two decades in the region. For being another Binayak Sen. Incredibly, all of this happened in a short span of less than six months. "People like us who enter the field of social activism, we enter it after proper thought and due deliberation," he tells me. "We know the consequences of our actions, we have no illusions."

I met Himanshu for the first time in July 2009, a few weeks after his Vanvasi Chetna Ashram (VCA) was destroyed in front of his young daughters' eyes. Alisha, his twelve-year-old asked him, "We help villagers, is that why our home is being torn down?" Haripriya, his seven-year-old was too stunned at the sight of the anti-mine vehicles, bulldozers, bullet-proof cars and a huge number of security men deployed to raze to the ground an ashram that gave shelter to countless people in need.

Himanshu, undefeated and undeterred, immediately set up shop in alternative rented accommodation in Dantewada itself. His temporary home is basically one large room with a double bed, a dining table and chairs, a bathroom tucked far away outside, and a verandah with a steel bed and mattress covered with a spotless white sheet and bolsters. This serves as his office, with a laptop connected to a battery charger on an extension board completing the rather surreal picture.

Just outside his house I can see a large tent. Himanshu informs me that this is ultimately the one place of refuge for tribal victims of injustice, whether it is rape or torture at the hands of the infamous Salwa Judum.

Himanshu advises me to visit the Salwa Judum camp at Dorna Pal first before I interview him about Binayak Sen. The distance is 114 odd kilometres but it will take me about five hours to go there and return to Dantewada before evening which is what he cautions me to do. He promises help from one of their VCA volunteers, giving me a mobile number along with the slightly alarming information that after Sukhma village, which is the mid-point to Dorna Pal, I would get no network at all. Luckily for me, the VCA volunteer (on a motorbike) tracks me down just before Sukhma and we reach the camp together, at Dorna Pal, his bike escorting my car all the way. And yet, the journey from Sukhma to Dorna Pal is one of the scariest I have undertaken, despite the fact that it was made in the middle of the afternoon!

Even the night before, at 10.30 pm, driving up to Jagdalpur on my way to Dantewada, in pouring rain, up a long and winding road, higher and higher up a hill with absolutely no other car in sight, I had felt faint stirrings of fear, not assuaged by the driver saying he hoped the car would not break down in the middle of "Naxal" territory.

But the next day's experience on the way to the Salwa Judum camp in Dorna Pal was definitely more frightening, or maybe the fear was more a creation of my mind, a fall-out of preconceived notions. Undoubtedly the landscape is breathtakingly beautiful, one of the best I have ever seen anywhere in the country—lush green land, leaves rustling in the cold breeze that blows over swaying trees, streams that are swollen to the size of small rivers due to the monsoons, clouds clearing now and then to display newly-washed clear blue skies—it is idyllic beyond belief. And incredibly silent.

The tarred road from Dantewada to Sukhma sees occasional traffic and some reassuring noise. After Sukhma, which is basically a small place with a few small shops, the route gets far more difficult. The road is narrower, full of pot-holes and bumps, and though the landscape is as alluring, travelling for miles on end without any sight or sound of another person or vehicle is a bit unnerving. A stray motor-cyclist, a solitary jeep, half-clad tribals carrying wood flash past.

Suddenly I am jolted by the sight of a posse of young men, perhaps fifteen in number, dressed in jeans and T-shirts, rifles casually slung across their shoulders, walking nonchalantly in the middle of the road. I am wide-eyed. "They are military people, they don't wear uniforms because of Naxalite terror in this area but everyone knows who they are," my driver informs me.

Finally we reach the Dorna Pal Salwa Judum camp. Row upon row of tin-roofed huts glinting in the afternoon sun, solid bamboo fencing, wood fires everywhere. An estimated 1885 tribal (mostly Gond) homes make up this four and a half year-old camp which runs like the government establishment it actually is—there is a school, a dispensary, food (rice and dal principally) is doled out to the inhabitants, hand-pumps for water, basic amenities all taken care of. I can even hear a radio in the distance.

Nikita Yadav, a young, bright-eyed and extremely helpful volunteer of the VCA, introduces me to as many people as are willing to talk to a perfect stranger about their lives (even less do on video, so I shut my camera off). Those that do talk, mostly toe a politically correct line, providing guarded answers. Sometimes, just here and there, a hint of honesty breaks through but I have to strain to catch it. Nikita tells me later that they do share their problems, their terror, their stories of victimization with the VCA, which most of them consider their strongest ally.

Being the "untrustworthy" outsider, I have to try hard to get a glimpse of what it means to live in a transit camp for almost five years, to be forced to leave one's home and long to return to it one day. And I discover that a lifetime will be too short to get the answers.

Purnim Rama of Dumbatola village near Sukhma road came to the camp three years ago, fed-up of constant harassment and Naxal terror. He feels secure in the camp since there is police patrolling day and night and though he wants to go back home one day, he thinks it a rather impossible dream and will stay put as long as the government keeps him. He is quite content with the facilities the camp offers him and his family. I try my knowledge of a few broken Gondi phrases culled from an earlier documentary made in Adilabad district but Purnim Rama refuses to share any more information.

I walk away to a woman sitting nearby. Her name is Muthai, and she is from Mervai village, roughly 12 kilometres away, where she says they used to live in constant fear of the Naxals. She feels safe in this camp where she has been living for the past three years. She does not want to talk to me any more either.

The VCA volunteer is apologetic but of course it is unrealistic to expect anyone to talk freely to a complete stranger in a closely guarded camp about totally unnatural, horrifying circumstances of displacement and upheaval.

Sariyam, a young teacher from the same village of Mervai, who has been living in the camp for four years, has old parents back home and visits them occasionally. He will go back if things improve and become more secure and says this may happen as it's not as frightening as it once was, at the time he fled his home. He too faces no difficulty at the camp, he assures me.

The next person I approach is also from Mervai. Sariambath, a young woman whose shy laughter punctuates her remarks at regular intervals, doesn't like life at the camp. There's no work to do here, just wasting time eating and sleeping, she says dismissively. The food too is just about tolerable, dal, rice, aloo, no *sabzi*. Life was infinitely better in their village, they used to farm there, they had a proper life there, they miss their families who have been left behind. From her chats with other women too, she knows they all want to go home, she confides. They came here only out of fear of the Naxals.

As I leave her and walk over to the huts opposite hers that have locks on them, her voice follows me, "They have left the camp...some forever, some to visit their relatives..." The wish to follow suit is unmistakable in her voice and stays with me as I continue to walk around.

Nikita is of invaluable help both as interpreter of the tribal Gondi language and as a familiar face they trust. I ask her to introduce me to old people in the camp who would remember similar experiences from the past. We meet Kanna from Vella village 20 kilometres away, who has been here for the last four and a half years. He came because the *sarpanch* of his village told him to, everyone else came here so he did too, his logic is simple. He wants to go back to his village, to die there, but has little hope of actually being able to do so. "I can only go if everyone else goes," he says fatalistically. In the village there was farming work to be done, fields to be ploughed. At the camp he rues the lack of work...his voice peters off while talking of camp facilities like food and medicines. He says he's seen similar (Naxal) activity before but is hard put to remember any details so we leave him to rest and approach the *mukhiya* of Theatreaiyka village, forty-five-year-old Madkamdeva, angry, articulate, animated.

"I came here four and a half years ago when our homes were destroyed. If I go back today, they (Naxals) will chop off my head. I have heard threats that they have issued to this effect, so how can I go home, you tell me! I have only one son, how will I be able to sleep there in my village peacefully even for one night? They used to roam around our village every day, we never did anything to them. People who returned home to the village were killed so we are better off staying here in the camp our entire lives. It's true that we have no work to do here and can't earn any money, there's no land to earn money but it's better to live here than die in the village. Many people think like me, that we will not survive if we go home. And we are not ungrateful, government gives us dal, rice, onions, houses, not *pukka* ones but they are still nice and we are secure here, police is here, schools, medicines, why should I lie about this?" he ends looking at me almost defiantly.

Tangram of Tetri village, 25 kilometres away, half his age, has a diametrically opposite view and is one of the rare ones who is unafraid to share it. He came here in 2006, again, due to the Naxal fear and was assured of security in the camp. But he claims he doesn't feel secure and wants to go back to his village and resume his life as he knew it—farming for a living. Reluctantly he adds that he will need the requisite amount of security to be able to do this, otherwise it will remain his dream and in the choice of freedom versus life, what *can* he choose?

There are other stories of other people who ask not to be named or photographed and I oblige, but even so, I rarely get a full picture.

By now it is almost 4.30 pm, well past Himanshu's dictum of my curfew time and Nikita and I head out of the camp, walking quickly, my camera hidden in a sling-bag, but no one asks any questions though security guards are everywhere. In July 2009 it is still possible for me to slip in and out of a Salwa Judum camp and shoot video camera footage and walk out unharmed.

The return journey is almost disappointingly uneventful but Himanshu's welcoming smile is like a beacon in the dusk descending over Dantewada. After ten minutes I wonder if that will actually be the sole source of light, as the electricity, never very reliable here, goes off suddenly and his house, like others in the surrounding area, is plunged into total darkness.

Himanshu relates an apocryphal tale that is so befitting his own situation here that I am rendered speechless. He is telling me the story to illustrate quite a different point, oblivious that it epitomizes him and his work. It is a simple tale by Rabindranath Tagore: One day the Sun, tired of always having to provide light to people, went to God and asked to be relieved of his responsibilities, just for a day's respite. God told the Sun to find Him an alternative and then he could go on leave. So the Sun went to the Moon and asked for one day's leave, asking the Moon to take its place, just for a day. The Moon refused, saying, how could it ever replace the brightness of the Sun? Not possible. The Sun then went to each and every star and got the same negative answer. Finally he went to a *diya* (earthen lamp) who answered, "I can't replace you or your brightness but I can guarantee that wherever I am, there will be no darkness."

For seventeen years, for thousands, perhaps even a few lakh tribals, Himanshu Kumar was the *diya* in Dantewada.

In the absence of any sun or moon or stars, he and his VCA volunteers stand committed to working for the well-being of the *adivasis* or tribals, even as they continue to face repeated, relentless harassment by a vindictive police force, a legal system that does not allow them to file FIRs, a government that wants them to stop the work they have been doing for the last seventeen years, a national media that just doesn't care to report what is happening. Apart from PUCL and associated activists, they have absolutely no other means of support. Himanshu gives the reason in two simple words: Salwa Judum. He also shares with me—at long last—confidences about Binayak Sen, a friend, a colleague, a person he admires.

Himanshu's definition of the Salwa Judum is simple and brutally forthright: "Salwa Judum is a way for corporate industrialists, corporate-funded, corporate-guided big-shots to get land vacated for mining purposes. In this venture, police forces and government attacked villages, got them vacated. They (government) thought Bastar is a remote area, nobody will get to know of this but the way Binayak and his team came here, investigated, went into great detail and exposed the truth about the Salwa Judum in their report, the government's plans were thwarted. I remember a very senior police officer telling me at that time that they would not spare the PUCL people."

But why single out Binayak alone, I ask? The reply is accompanied by his trademark smile. "Binayak Sen does work relentlessly, without stopping, on a daily basis. Other people do work once in a while. That's his nature. Now that he is out of jail, he will raise up a storm again!"

I query whether the price Binayak paid for doing this work was too high and Himanshu laughs, "For an activist to spend a year or two in jail is not a very big thing, it's in fact a reward! It's a small price to pay, he may have to pay a far higher price in future."

He goes on to add that such acts on the part of governments, arrests or demolitions that are meant as deterrents actually don't work on some people. "They think they can destroy our homes, put us in jail, scare us, threaten us and then we will stop talking about Salwa Judum? The opposite happens, people like us and Binayak, we fight with greater vigour and strength. The greater the oppression, the stronger the worker. I live in Dantewada and I raise these issues every day and I didn't get scared."

In Binayak's case too, Himanshu feels that the two-year jail term, far from suppressing the issue, brought it upfront, into the limelight. Many more people got to know about it, got involved in it, and now, in the days to come, Binayak will play a major role in the fight against the way governments are dealing with adivasis, dalits, minorities, treating them like second-class citizens. Himanshu vows to "fight a good fight" with his friend Binayak, to help society get rid of these evils.

Binayak was a regular visitor to the VCA and a friend much before the Salwa Judum came into existence, recalls Himanshu, staying at their ashram, working, interacting with them. Then, after April 2005, when the Salwa Judum started its operations, Binayak came to Dantewada as part of a fourteen member team from five national organizations that conducted a fact-finding investigation, visited the area, interviewed the villagers, the displaced tribals, went to the Salwa Judum camps (like the one at Dorna Pal that I visited), interacted with Naxalites and government officials and presented their report. In all of this, the VCA helped them enormously.

Himanshu talks of being fascinated and influenced by one particular aspect of Binayak's personality. "He would never get angry. No matter how serious or enormous the issue, he would state his point of view very calmly but effectively. His words would carry weight. I used to be very impressed by his style—something that arouses such anger and yet he can present it so calmly, he speaks softly but the *himmat* with which he works, I have seen in him a *deewangi*, a passion," he says admiringly.

Himanshu is drawing a portrait of a revolutionary, someone who, once he's convinced something is wrong, goes after it like a possessed person, setting it right or trying to, meeting people, creating awareness through discussions, taking up every issue as a revolution. "In Bastar, when Salwa Judum started, Binayak went after it and brought it into the limelight in such a clear manner that the government was put in a spot and framed false charges against him and jailed him. It's indicative of how impressively he would have done his work and presented his case that the government was forced to jail him," says Himanshu.

~

On May 25, 2009, standing outside Raipur Jail and facing the media on the day of his release on bail, Binayak vowed to continue his campaign against the Salwa Judum. He termed the Salwa Judum a major threat to peace, a source of oppression and pledged not only the PUCL's but his own personal opposition to it. This inspite of the fact that his exposé of the Salwa Judum through a report entitled "When the State Makes War On Its Own People" was one of the major underlying reasons the state government had imprisoned him.

However, the fact remains that though the Salwa Judum has become the symbol of everything that is unjust in the state of Chhattisgarh today, more specifically in Bastar and Dantewada districts, the story of human rights abuse began much earlier. As did Binayak's documentation of it, as a PUCL activist and defender of human rights. His aim was to ensure that future abuse was halted. Taking on the state police head-on was not on his agenda but could not have been avoided since he was the General Secretary of the PUCL, therefore a prime target. But he's glad today that the issue of human rights has been highlighted through his case because without such strong responses human rights defenders will remain vulnerable.

Here are some of the markers in Binayak's journey that led to his later exposé of the Salwa Judum:

Land acquisition—Nagarnar, Bastar, March 2002
According to the PUCL team's findings, villagers were compelled to accept compensation cheques and give up their

land in favour of the proposed Nagarnar Steel Plant, under "force and fear". Two hundred and fifty villagers were jailed. Villagers also confirmed police beatings and destruction of houses. The required permission of the Gram Sabha that is mandatory in such land acquisition deals was willfully ignored in this and other similar instances in the region. Binayak himself witnessed 85 of the 250 detenues being brought to the court in a bus. With handcuffs on, they were kept waiting for six hours and served warrants without any charges being explained to them.

Death in police custody—Sarguja, August 2003

The police called it an encounter death and termed Prasidhi Thakur a Zonal Commander of the Naxalite organization, the Maoist Communist Centre or MCC. Binayak conducted research in Khori village, talking to people who told the committee that it appeared to be a death in police custody. None of the provisions of the DK Basu Protocol were adhered to in the arrest of Prasidhi Thakur. This protocol relates to the statutory provisions regarding arrest and detention.

Electoral fraud—Dantewada district, April 2004

A PUCL team conducted extensive field research in Dantewada district, Bastar, on polling day to find polling booths missing. The villagers said that they had never seen booths in their area. Amazingly, votes supposedly cast at these booths—Gachchanpalli, Kollaiguda and Pentapad—had been counted!

Police encounter—Gollapalli, November 2004

Concerned over the contradictory reports in the media in the first week of November 2004 regarding the death of three persons in supposed cross firing between security forces and the Naxalites *and* a police encounter, in Gollapalli village of Konta tehsil in Dantewada district, Binayak along with a fact-finding team investigated the incident, including testimonies of the witnesses on video-camera (This was done by Pranhita, her first exposure to the kind of work her father was involved in.). Binayak and the team found and interviewed the only surviving victim of the "crossfire", Santosh Kumar Thakur, a teacher (Shiksha Karmi) who had sustained bullet injuries and who described what happened on 5 November:

Every evening the teachers and students played cricket together and that evening Santosh Thakur, his colleague Malla Ram Markam and a twelve-year-old student from Class 7, Hapka Nagendra, heard the sound of a blast. They ran into the teacher's headquarters, shut the doors and windows, listening in terror to the voices of the Chhattisgarh armed forces asking them to come out or face dire consequences. Pleas that they were only teachers and not Naxalites went unheeded as armed men surrounded the house, SAF jawans began firing. Sodhi Hidma, a young Sanvida Shikshak (a teacher on contract) died on the spot, so did Hapka Nagendra. The injured teacher Malla Ram Markam was taken to the police station in Gollapalli and died because he did not receive medical help in time. Santosh Thakur's statement categorically denying any cross firing by Naxalites, and specifying the deaths of his two students due to close range firing by SAF personnel and deliberate medical negligence in the case of Malla Ram Markam, was recorded by the *Sarpanch* of Gollapalli village and submitted to the *tehsildar*, Konta, the next morning. Other eye witnesses who met Binayak corroborated Santosh's story but the official version, a statement issued by the Inspector General of Police, continues to be that three persons were killed in a Naxalite-police "crossfire". No FIR was registered on the basis of the testimony of the sole surviving victim of the Gollapalli deaths, Santosh Kumar Thakur.

Deaths in police custody

The list of names that figured in the PUCL's investigations into deaths in police custody is a long one, beginning with Sunhar Nishad in January 1999. From then on, the grim roll call is recorded in black and white in the PUCL files and folders, their own database of human rights excesses: Shiv Kumar, Bhagwanta Sahu, Baldau Kaushik, Ram Kumar Dhruv, Sukhlal Lodhi, Bannu Ram Satnami, Naresh Das...

Names of women who have been raped by uniformed policemen inside police *thanas*...even as one name morphs into another and another, not even registering properly after a while, due to the sheer number and the callousness of the abuse, for the human rights workers, for people like Binayak, these were not just names to be forgotten. These were people whose battles had to be fought, in solidarity.

And so, painstakingly, complaints were recorded, FIRs were either filed or sought to be filed, statements were provided to *tehsildars*, information and eye-witness accounts were gathered and filed away as documentation for future reference. All part of the activist's, if not strictly the doctor's role.

Sudha Bhardwaj of the CMM, family friend and lawyer, puts it succinctly: "I think Doc Saab did exactly what a person with a conscience would do, what a civil liberties activist would do. It went against his grain to be aggressive but it also went against his grain to tolerate such injustice. He uncovered the silent war that had been going on in Chhattisgarh." Sudha is referring to the Salwa Judum.

While researching and documenting illegalities by the state machinery, including those perpetrated by the security forces, from almost the very inception of the state of Chhattisgarh in 2000 and doing their development work related to Rupantar that included the state-sponsored community health worker

Mitanin programme, Binayak and Ilina seem to have led lives which were on parallel tracks. And yet there was no apparent conflict till April 2005, the year that the Salwa Judum was formed, ostensibly to contain the Naxalite threat in Bastar.

As General Secretary of the Chhattisgarh PUCL, Binayak wrote an impassioned appeal in November 2005, outlining the suppression of human rights in the state, beginning with displacement due to projects like dams, factories, express highways, exploitation of natural resources of forests, minerals, land and water. He decried the fact that many industries such as the Bhilai Steel Plant (BSP), National Thermal Power Corporation (NTPC), Bharat Aluminium Corporation (BALCO) and Jindal Steel and Power (JSP) used contractual systems where deaths and industrial injuries were very common.

But far more importantly, his objective was to spread awareness about the "mass awakening" campaign being carried out in the Bastar region of the state under the banner of Salwa Judum, a supposedly spontaneous peaceful people's uprising against Naxalite violence.

In his published appeal, Binayak shared his and the PUCL's concerns that this "spontaneous peaceful people's uprising against Naxalite violence" enjoyed the joint patronage of the state government, the state unit of the BJP, the leader of the opposition in the State Assembly, sections of the Congress party, the State Police and the Central Reserve Police Force (CRPF). He also recorded the fact that there was a phenomenal increase in the Police and CRPF presence recently in Bastar, especially Dantewada, including the notorious Naga battalion.

Binayak then raised pertinent questions about the "non-violent nature" of the Salwa Judum, more so as media reports were based on police sources. Only some independent reports (Manish Kunjam, Jansatta, NDTV) came up with shocking stories: that people were being compelled to join the Salwa Judum rallies by brute force and those refusing to do so have their homes destroyed and their crops burnt. Youngsters in particular were being terrorized to join the Salwa Judum rallies. If they didn't, they were tagged as Naxalite supporters and tortured and sometimes even killed.

In November 2005 when Binayak published this appeal, he quoted one report that claimed that more than 12,000 villagers had been displaced from their villages and lodged in police protected camps in the name of security. Where each family was given one tent to live, to sleep on the wet ground protected only by a rubber sheet, inadequate drinking water, no electricity, no health facilities and food given by the police. Binayak added an urgent appeal to his note, asking all human rights organizations, all democratic forces to join hands in investigating the reality of the Salwa Judum, a national level team to counter what he termed the "mainstream media's present role of propagating the government viewpoint alone".

Not surprisingly, within a month, a fourteen-member team from five organizations was formed, which conducted its investigation in the Bijapur and Bhairamgarh blocks of Dantewada district in Bastar from November 28 to December 1, 2005. Binayak Sen was a part of this team, which interviewed villagers, Naxalites, officials in the area and brought out in April 2006, a 42-page report called "When the State Makes War on Its Own People". The report is exhaustive, providing a socio-economic background of Dantewada, the region, the tribals, their dependence on the forests, the irony of how the people of Dantewada are extremely poor while their land is extremely rich, both in terms of minerals and forests.

And this of course is the crux of all the agony that Dantewada's displaced tribals continue to endure—exploitation of their resources for private profit, industrial development and export, clearing of their land, their villages to make way for development, for MOUs signed with large corporates. Binayak's November PUCL appeal mentions MOUs for an investment of Rs 17,000 crore signed for the proposed Tata and Essar Steel Plants in Bastar alone. Many of these development projects are achievable only at the cost of the destruction of tribal livelihood systems, writes Binayak, and as such, tribal resistance is only to be anticipated.

The report is a meticulous and searing indictment of the lack of governance in predominantly tribal Dantewada (37 police stations as against 26 primary health centers and 26 higher secondary schools, lowest literacy level in the entire country, starvation deaths, lack of potable water and health care) and an unflinching, no-holds-barred exposé of the Salwa Judum—its origins, its way of functioning, its supporters and their goals.

A brief excerpt from the report provides a chilling account of the modus operandi of the Salwa Judum:

> "...Salwa Judum meetings are called, people from neighbouring villages are asked to be present. On that date, a Salwa Judum crowd accompanied by security forces descends on the village and asks people to come to the camp and *sangham* (Naxalite or Maoist) members to surrender. Heavy security forces accompany the meetings. Audiences for these meetings are transported in buses hired by the administration. If villagers show reluctance, they are attacked, belongings looted, houses burnt and sometimes people are killed by soldiers... No FIR is ever registered for those killed by security forces. People from defeated villages are then forced to come and live in the camps (of which the administration itself claims to have set up 17), unable to continue with their agricultural activities and their normal existence...

Across Dantewada and Bijapur police districts and especially all along the national highway, security forces and Salwa Judum members man checkpoints. The Salwa Judum question people, check their belongings and even enjoy the power to stop a person from travelling in this area..."

At the conclusion of their report, the PUCL and Binayak asked for all killings—by the state, the Salwa Judum and the Maoists—to be stopped, for the paramilitary forces to be withdrawn from the area, for the camps to be dismantled and people assisted in regaining their livelihoods in their villages, for a sincere dialogue to be initiated with the Maoists and a political resolution to the situation to be found.

That was in April 2006.

None of their demands were met.

Instead, Binayak was arrested and imprisoned for two years from May 14, 2007 till May 25, 2009.

The immediate trigger for the arrest was believed to be the PUCL's repeated and public demands for an inquiry into the fake encounter deaths of twelve civilians at Santoshpur in Bijapur district in Chhattisgarh. In fact the PUCL state convention held on April 14 and 15 in Ambikapur had as its theme, "Fake Encounters, Fake Surrenders and Fake Cases".

Bastar then proceeded to become a battleground, 40,000 square km of land being guarded by 20 battalions of paramilitary forces 6000 local policemen in addition to the dreaded SPOs (Special Police Officers often culled from the Salwa Judum).

Three and a half lakh villagers have been displaced since 2005, of which almost one lakh have migrated to Andhra Pradesh and Maharashtra. Approximately 40,000 are living in the camps and the rest are hiding in the jungles. There are no records for the missing and dead. They remain unaccounted for. As do the women who have been raped. Other than magazine articles recording their agony there is nobody they could turn to for aid. Despite Himanshu Kumar's VCA filing more than 600 complaints against the Salwa Judum over the last five years, not one FIR could be lodged. Himanshu himself rues the fact that he could not obtain justice from the courts for even one tribal in the last five years.

The Supreme Court passed an order based on Delhi-based activist and professor Nandini Sundar's petition to rehabilitate all villages destroyed by the Salwa Judum. Till May 2010, nothing has been done in this regard. Instead the government launched Operation Greenhunt in Bastar to "clear" the area of Maoist control.

Binayak continues to speak against the Salwa Judum at public platforms, at lectures, at seminars, at informal gatherings, uncaring of personal consequences. "Once you are a part of the human rights movement and I am part of a very large movement, there are people paying a major price for taking part in these issues, so many people have been killed as a result of their peaceful, non-violent efforts in the area of human rights, it's nothing new. At the point of decision you don't start making choices, your choices have been made a long time ago," he says when I ask him about the dangers involved in going down this path. By virtue of the fact that neutrality is not a luxury that is available to everyone, that silence is not an alternative, someone had to do it, that someone in this case was him.

In his own words, the decision had been made a long time ago— perhaps as far back as his student days while pursuing his post-graduation thesis in malnutrition in paediatrics when he visited the homes of his young patients, to determine the socio-economic causes that did not allow some children to ever get well again.

The starting point of health as an inalienable human right, the more visibly political interventions in Dalli Rajhara with trade union workers, followed by his own socio-politcal network of community health and education voluntary organization (Rupantar), all of it running parallel to his activities as a PUCL activist, would have made it almost impossible for a person of his nature to ignore what was happening right in front of him.

The die had been cast almost thirty years ago, and today Binayak Sen is coping with both sides of the coin, the trials and tribulations as well as the fame and admiration. Characteristically he chooses to deal with both with equal equanimity, concentrating instead on his agenda for "peace, justice and equity", the only solutions he has to offer at this time, for the troubled times in his troubled state.

Chapter Eight

THE TRIAL: PAST AND PRESENT

Raipur

What can you say about a trial that perhaps never should have seen the light of day at all, given that almost every person I discuss it with, lawyers at every end of the spectrum, activists of every hue and leaning, even government officials who naturally refuse to be quoted, but freely admit that "there isn't much of a case really".

So why and for whom ultimately, is this almost Kafka-esque posturing, the insistence on strict adherence to procedural formalities, the long-drawn out due process of the law, the four-month long testimonies of a single witness, despite the avowed "fast track court"?

No one knows and no one really cares.

~

Court Number 11 at the trial court premises, Raipur, is easily identified. All I have to do is mention Binayak Sen to the swarm of lawyers dressed in flapping black coats and they immediately direct me to it. I reach ten minutes before the stipulated time of 11 am on September 16, 2009, for the monthly date of the continuing trial of Dr Binayak Sen in the fast track court of Justice Balvinder Singh Saluja. A trial that began on April 30, 2008 with a 1000 page chargesheet (two more chargesheets have been subsequently filed) and 153 witnesses, is now losing steam fast.

Sixteen witnesses were supposed to testify in the three days allotted for September's trial dates. Only five showed up. Today's roll call is an expected sum total of two witnesses. No one stops or checks me as I enter the nondescript building and sit on a bench alongside the wall, in the long, narrow, empty corridor just outside a door which bears the judge's name and a signboard, *Chhattisgarh Rajya Nyayik Karmachari Sangh-Prantiya Zila Karyalaya*, Raipur.

An occasional gust of breeze causes the dirty old curtain to fly, giving me glimpses of the interior of the court room. I can see medium-sized steel cupboards. A sari-clad lady official flanked by two policemen walks past, opening doors, switching on lights. Another official carrying bulky papers covered in yellow cloth and all bound together settles inside and thus, the instruments for delivering justice for this day are duly laid out, for the representatives of the judicial system to do their part—the Public Prosecutor and the Judge. It will take a further hour and a half at least, for both to make an appearance.

But at 11 am exactly, armed with a bottle of mineral water and a book and a handkerchief, standard staples for a long day ahead, Binayak enters, dressed in a crisp long kurta and white pyjama, hair neatly combed back, courteous smile and manners in place, brother Deepanker in tow and sits next to me on the bench. This is quite obviously familiar ground for him and he humours Deepanker and me with stories about completely different topics, perhaps to deflect our growing impatience at the delay.

And thus, almost as a bonus, I witness at close quarters, (quite literally), a side of Binayak I had never seen till then, someone who seemed far more keenly attuned to human nature and emotions than the rather self-contained, almost aloof exterior that is exhibited to others most of the time. The aloofness isn't at all impolite. On the contrary, Binayak is a very gentle man, he will go out of his way to welcome you, put you at ease. But the distance, while not overtly visible, is there. This is a man who wishes to be left alone to continue his work, his thought processes, to just be by himself...

But that day on that bench outside Court 11, Binayak, in an expansive mood, is on a roll. He talks about how important it is for any socialist to have love and anger within him. Only love and no anger will lead to nothing—no aim, no goal. Only anger will lead to bitterness—again, no larger goal. So a blend of both is best, he nods at Deepanker and me. I listen carefully, trying to decipher the hidden meanings of his reasons for telling us this right now. I give up in about ten minutes.

Binayak then softly sings a song in a low, yet tuneful voice. All I can remember of the lines are "I asked the Captain the time but the Captain threw away the watch..." Binayak sings at least four verses. Seamlessly I find myself asking him about his known love for music and he mentions predictable names—Janice Joplin, Joan Baez, Eric Clapton, the Beatles as well. Omissions are the Rolling Stones, Led Zeppelin, Pink Floyd, The Doors, and Deepanker and I tell him about a Pink Floyd live performance in Pompeii, available on DVD. Deepanker says, "Dada, we'll do a trip together to Pompeii," and Binayak answers in turn, on a slightly sobering note, "Whenever I'm able to get my visa."

For people who are engaged always in work to be disengaged for so long is difficult, he says, wanting to go back to his Bagrumnala clinic that has been waiting for him for more than two years. Apart from the medical work that is on hold for the moment, there's lots for him to do, he informs me. He is writing about Salwa Judum, an article for Antara Dev Sen's "The Little Magazine", another one for the "Lancet". He has to deliver the Chandrashekhar Memorial Lecture in Patna, then another in Mumbai, Delhi, go to Vellore...there is no dearth of tasks to be completed.

What is left unsaid is most telling. What has really been taken away from Binayak Sen is his freedom to do what he wants to do *when* and *how* and as *many times* he wants to do it, whether it is visiting his patients at the Bagrumnala clinic or going back on his investigation trails of the Salwa Judum. The freedom to do all and any of this without fear of reprisal or intimidation.

The morning crosses over to afternoon and even as Binayak quietly drinks his bottled water and reads his book, I alternately pace the now bustling corridor and stare at his calm, unruffled profile, till he glances up and smiles. "Sit down, you don't look very well," he admonishes me.

"Give her some money please," he requests his brother and only then do we realize that an old beggar lady has been quietly standing near us. She accepts ten rupees gratefully and goes away. Only Binayak noticed her.

Later, emboldened by this little bit of byplay, a snake-charmer approaches Binayak asking for money to feed his snake milk and is gently shooed away. All that Binayak says is, "People in misery seek ways to propitiate the gods any way they can."

At the end of ninety minutes it seems almost an anti-climax to finally enter Court 11. Binayak tells Deepanker and I to go in separately since he will be going into the accused box and with that simple instruction I am reminded with a shock that he is to be demarcated here from everyone else present. He is the accused and we are all free people while he is only free on bail, which can be revoked at any time.

The white-haired, elderly Public Prosecutor enters the court room. Binayak stands up as a sign of respect because "this man represents the authority that is supposed to provide justice," or at least that is the answer he provides his brother who is furious with the Prosecution's version of events as the trial unfolds.

Only one witness for the prosecution has turned up for the entire day, a police inspector, I H Khan, who proceeds to give his testimony in a barely audible voice for the next three hours. His monotone seems rehearsed and after a while the defence lawyer, Mahendra Dubey, part of Binayak's team, raises this objection, accusing Khan of being tutored by his superiors, of saying things that were not on record. The judge, perched on a high chair, calmly asks the typist sitting below him to record the objection on the computer, dictating the words slowly.

The court room is what one imagines a court room to be, given stereotypes handed down through cinema or television, the only difference being its size and shabbiness. There are two benches for visitors, one for the battery of black-robed lawyers (there are six for this case), two glass-topped tables at either end of the room, steel cupboards lining the edges, and the mandatory witness and accused box, where currently Binayak is sitting along with second and third accused Narayan Sanyal and Piyush Guha.

Apart from a few interjections and objections from the defence counsel, where voices are raised and the dispassionate demeanour of the judge is ruffled to an extent, and Binayak is roused sufficiently enough to stand up in order to listen more carefully, the proceedings drag on and on, interminably. For the most part, Binayak sits quietly in the accused box, observing the goings-on, chatting with Narayan Sanyal occasionally. He has done this for almost two years now, first while he was in jail and now each month, interrupting his life whenever he is summoned to mark attendance in this courtroom.

Around 4 pm it is all over for the day and also, for the month of September 2009. The six lawyers, the judge, the witness, the three accused and the office staff all troop out. Just before that, the next trial date is fixed for the following month.

We all walk out of the court's premises with different responses to the day. Deepanker is annoyed that only three-odd hours of testimony have been recorded in the entire working day. Binayak characteristically, does not reveal much of what he is feeling and in any case, he is accustomed to such delay tactics over the last eighteen months and knows he has to face many more, while I will probably never see this court room again and am still processing the day in my mind.

This personal experience of the trial on Sept 16, 2009 is a toned-down, sanitized version in sharp contrast to the volatile situation that existed in the initial days of the trial, given all I had read and heard others describe of the atmosphere of intentional intimidation in 2008 when Binayak was in jail and used to be produced in court for the trial hearings. Apart from family members like Ilina and friends like Kavita Shrivastava, Sudha Bhardwaj or Chhattisgarh PUCL President Rajendra Sail, all of whom personally witnessed this scenario, month after month, other trial observers were from the Medico Friends Circle, or MFC, like Dr Abhay Shukla who had equally alarming reports to share such as this one based on his observations at the August 25, 2008 trial hearing:

> "There was an overwhelming presence of the police in the court premises and outside the court room. The main entrance gate remains closed throughout the trial. Sniffer dogs and mine-sensing equipments are used to search the entire court premises. Every person attending the trial is first interviewed

by the Inspector, asking details about identity, address, contact details, purpose of visit and relationship with the accused. An entry of these details is made in a book maintained by the Information Officer or IO. The person attending the trial is then thoroughly searched by security personnel posted outside the courtroom and then sniffed by the dog before being allowed to enter. No hand bags are allowed to be carried inside the courtroom and have to be left outside. The Court remains a silent spectator to this."

Such precautionary measures are normally used for hardened criminals or terrorists. But the formal court chargesheet actually accuses Binayak Sen of waging war against the state, creating a conspiracy, aiding and abetting treason against the Government of India, participating in illegal activities in illegal organizations, conducting and addressing meetings of terrorist organizations to increase their activities…this is the language used in the February 2, 2008 chargesheet issued by Additional Sessions Judge B S Saluja, read and signed by accused Binayak Sen but denied by him as totally baseless.

In legalese, Binayak Sen has been charged for offences under 121a,124a,120b of the Indian Penal Code (IPC), Sections 3,10, 20, 21, 38, 39 of the Unlawful Activities [Prevention]Act 2004, Sections 2,8[1][2][3][5] of the Chhattisgarh Special Public Securities Act 2005. To put it more simply, Binayak has been charged with supporting the activities of the CPI (Maoist), meeting a jailed Naxalite leader Narayan Sanyal thirty three times in one year, and for acting as a courier for Sanyal by carrying material, notably incriminating letters, through a businessman, Piyush Guha, known to have Naxalite links. This trio—the police term of endearment for Sanyal, Sen and Guha—was supposed to be working together to "create a negative feeling about the established government, conspiring against it to commit serious and dangerous crimes, to spread terror, violence, bomb blasts and destroy electricity towers and railway lines, with the mastermind being Narayan Sanyal." To quote the first chargesheet, "Narayan Sanyal is a Naxalite mastermind at whose behest electric towers have been blown up in Bastar and the whole area put in darkness. Sanyal, through Binayak Sen and Piyush Guha, is involved in violent activities and propaganda in Naxalite areas."

Narayan Sanyal was and is a senior level functionary of the Politburo of the Maoist (CPI) party, Piyush Guha is a businessman who is also alleged to have Naxalite links and Binayak Sen, in his capacity as PUCL General Secretary visited Sanyal in jail in Raipur thirty three times in a year (supervised visits, under the watchful eye of the jailor or his assistant) for the purpose of providing Sanyal medical treatment and legal advice. As for clandestine meetings with Piyush Guha in seedy hotels in Raipur in order to pass on documents for onward distribution to banned Naxalite organizations, despite every attempt (by the prosecution) to corroborate such meetings, not a single witness has been able to identify seeing Binayak and Piyush Guha together.

The last part of the prosecution's case is the "objectionable" material found in the computer CPU and the eight CDs seized from Binayak's home in Surya Apartments, in the search and seizure exercise conducted by the police, five days after he was arrested. The objectionable matter or evidence against Binayak is this:

o A post-card dated June 3, 2006, written to Binayak by Narayan Sanyal from Raipur Central Jail, regarding his health as well as legal case, duly signed by the jail authorities and with the jail seal

o A yellow coloured booklet titled "On the Unity Between CPI (People's War) and Maoist Communist Centre" in Hindi o A letter written by Madanlal Banjare (a member of the CPI-Maoist) from jail addressed to "*priya* Comrade Binayak Sen"

o A xeroxed article in English entitled "Naxal Movement, Tribals and Women's Movement"

o A handwritten, photocopied note of four pages on "How to Build an Anti-US Imperialist Front"

o An eight-page article entitled: "Krantikari Janwadi Morcha (ITF) (Revolutionary People's Front) Vaishavikaran Awam Bahrtiye Seva Kshetra (Globalization and the Service Sector in India)

That is the entire case, in a nutshell, the sum total of the offences Binayak is alleged to have committed against the state, which are deemed "seditious" in nature.

The first chargesheet minces no words in its description of Binayak, just as it did with Narayan Sanyal. The words often contradict themselves though:

o Dr Binayak Sen believes in the Naxalite ideology, is hand-in-glove with the Naxalites, is an active Naxalite and directly and indirectly communicating information to Naxalites in the field.

o Dr Sen is certainly a doctor, but is a big zero in terms of actual practice of medicine. During the search of his house, no material as would be found in a clinic or any medicines were found.

o On examination of sources of funds, it was found that he does not have any legitimate source of income.

o It is a matter of common discussion in Raipur and in surrounding areas that Dr Sen and his wife Ilina Sen receive foreign funds to help Naxalites.

o Dr Sen's medical activities are only a mask and using this mask he tours the Naxalite areas. All his work is meant to help Naxalites. It is under this mask that all his illegal activities are going on and he projects himself as a doctor in the media.

I described the contents and wording of this chargesheet to Binayak's patients at Bagrumnala and heard him described in turn as God by them, someone who has cured a son, a daughter, a wife, a family member of all kinds of illnesses. The "fake doctor" charge arouses immense anger amongst Binayak's patients.

The supplementary chargesheet filed in December 2008 includes details of bank accounts and a charitable trust set up by Binayak and Ilina in 1995, a letter from the computer hard disk that details the need for human rights intervention in the worsening situation in Chhattisgarh and since the letter begins with "my dear..." it is presented as sinister, with "my dear..." suspected to being some sort of code!

Additionally the chargesheet contains news clippings which detail loss of life and destruction in Naxalite attacks, and news clippings on how the National Human Rights Commission (NHRC) gave a clean chit to the Salwa Judum.

A third chargesheet filed in August 2009 basically relates to other Naxalite cases, mentions various (seemingly) irrelevant documents related to income tax details and telephone calls for Rupantar.

A fourth chargesheet followed, containing details of telephone calls, nothing that could be considered relevant in terms of criminal law, to provide even remote assistance to the prosecution in bringing home the alleged charges for which Binayak is being prosecuted.

The obvious and not even hidden agenda is to prolong the case as much as possible, and in Indian courts that truly can be a long, long time. The prosecution has cited 153 witnesses in their case, 95 have been examined till March 2010 with the case having progressed not much further since. Since Binayak cannot discuss the case as long as it is in court, I ask Ilina when they can expect a verdict and she shrugs helplessly. The testimony of one sub-inspector has been going on since December 2009, she tells me in March 2010, so how can anyone predict the time frame, leave alone the outcome of a trial of this nature?

In the meantime, the lives of the Sen family, at least of Binayak and Ilina, (the girls are busy studying and working outside Chhattisgarh) are adjusted to suit the timetable of the trial court dates each month and they have come to terms with it, for as long as it will take. Today at least they are together, facing the possibility of more chargesheets. Two and a half years ago, in 2007, Ilina had to fight many battles alone albeit with the support of friends and fellow workers and ultimately from total strangers as well!

The nightmare began the day Binayak was arrested in Bilaspur on May 14, 2007. Binayak had gone to Kalyani in West Bengal to meet his mother and had a clear indication through activist friends that he might be arrested once he returned to Raipur. Many of them, including old colleagues in Vellore advised him not to return but Binayak being Binayak, he chose to come back.

He was visiting Sudha Bhardwaj in Bilaspur when he was told by a policeman that the police wished to record his statement. Both Sudha and Binayak went to the Tar Bahar police station to do so, where they were told that a formal arrest would be made by a team from the Raipur police. Binayak was then arrested, medically examined, produced before the court of the Chief Judicial Magistrate, Bilaspur and then sent to jail. Bail was denied.

Three days later, on May 18, Binayak was produced in court, a search warrant for his house was ordered, no incriminating material was found.

By this time, multiple protest rallies, meetings and letters of support had started pouring in from all corners of the country and the world, starting with Amnesty International the very next day (May 15), to delegations of doctors and human rights activists meeting the Chief Secretary and other dignitaries both in the state and at the Centre.

On May 25, bail was denied again on the grounds that Binayak was a threat to state security.

On June 5 Binayak had his day in court and rebutted all the police allegations. Two days later, Ilina sent a submission to the NHRC stating that no chargesheet had been filed against Binayak thus far, and protesting the mala fide intentions of the state of Chhattisgarh in first identifying its victims and then seeking to build up concocted cases against them. The first chargesheet was finally filed by the police on August 3, 2007.

It was a fight on every count, every step of the way and there was perhaps no time to even get tired. Ilina had to simultaneously deal with the lawyers and the twists and turns of the case as well as mobilize public opinion and support for her husband. It didn't help that the state made it as hard as possible, at one time not producing Binayak in court as ordered, citing the lack of the necessary armed escort for a "dangerous criminal" as a reason. The distance from the jail to the court is not more than 2 kilometres.

Binayak's defence lawyers would not get access to routine courtesies like the FIR that was initially lodged, while the analysis of his computer, conducted by the CFSL in Hyderabad in their absence, compelled them to lodge a protest. Witnesses would not turn up (and still don't today) on specified days of the trial, delaying the process further.

Despite this being a public trial, before Binayak was released on bail, each and every visitor inside the courtroom was checked and interrogated, with a heavy security presence outside the court room complete with the sniffer dogs. This noticeably harsh treatment was also a major reason for the appointment of external trial observers like MFC's Abhay Shukla, whose presence acted as a positive check on the court, reinforcing the message that there was a much larger public interest in the trial. It also boosted the morale of Binayak's family members and lawyers who were, at that point, confronting a very oppressive situation in Chhattisgarh. Most importantly, such continued trial observation and publicizing of any irregularities on a wide scale is the only tool available to ensure that a trial of a human rights defender does not lead to conviction on falsely constructed grounds.

Such a situation actually came true much later, on July 29, 2008 when tampering of evidence was brought to light during the examination of Shyam Sunder Rao, a prosecution witness to the seizure and search of Binayak's house in Raipur. The list of ten items in the seizure list mysteriously included an eleventh one at the eleventh hour, a photocopied letter from a member of the CPI (Maoist) addressed to Binayak, thanking him for his assistance. It did not bear Binayak's signature however, found no mention in the seizure memo and was not part of the original chargesheet.

Defence lawyer Mahendra Dubey immediately raised an objection to allowing this letter to be included as evidence but the objection was not recorded by the court. The witness, when asked about this mysterious letter had no explanation to offer.

It was to pre-empt and highlight precisely such acts of questionable, unethical behaviour that organizations such as the Commonwealth Human Rights Initiative, or CHRI, and the European Union, or EU, delegations sent their representatives to Raipur to observe the trial of Binayak Sen. Nawaz Kotwal monitored the trial on behalf of the CHRI, while a French and a Dutch diplomat from the EU delegation came to India but their trial observation reports could never be made public since the state government accused the members of being Naxal supporters and claimed they did not have the requisite permission to move out of Delhi.

While the July 2007 High Court bail petition for Binayak was rejected on the grounds that the police had incriminating evidence from Binayak's hard disc (evidence that is yet to be proved in any manner) on December 10, 2007, a two-judge bench of the Supreme Court denied Binayak's bail petition after just 35 minutes of deliberation.

Even as Binayak and the family dealt with the blow of the Supreme Court's rejection of the bail petition, the next blow was equally unexpected. Binayak was sent into solitary confinement from March 15 to April 11, 2008 and given absolutely no reason beyond that of his own security. Widespread protests from friends and activists finally rescued him and his trial began on April 30, 2008, with defence lawyers Ram Jethmalani, Shanti Bhushan, Rajeev Dhawan, Mahendra Dubey, and Anjana Prakash continuing their efforts to get him out of jail.

A second bail petition in the Chhattisgarh High Court followed in August 2008. The hearing got adjourned. A second bail petition in the Supreme Court was also opposed in December 2008, on technical grounds, since there was no fresh ground from the previous bail rejection and also because the hearings are going on "expeditiously and will lead to an early and expeditions conclusion of the trial." The irony of these words, "early and expeditious conclusion of the trial" is undoubtedly harder for those close to Binayak to endure.

Sudha Bhardwaj is openly skeptical about the outcome of the case. "Legally, there was nothing in the case right from the beginning, and there is nothing remaining in it. They are trying to add some *masala*, some hearsay. Dirty tricks are also being used, witnesses are improving on their statements. It was always a politically motivated trial and we hope ultimately truth will prevail but it's not difficult to imagine victory will be under a lot of pressure."

In the end it was relentless pressure from support groups comprising a concerted Free Binayak Sen campaign, locally, nationally and internationally that combined to free Binayak from jail, almost two years to the day he was arrested and on May 25, 2009, the Supreme Court finally granted him unconditional bail (on a personal bond) in less than sixty seconds, the judge declaring in a one-line sentence that it was two years too much.

That same afternoon Binayak walked out of Central Jail, Raipur, dressed in his trademark kurta-pyjama, raising his hand in a victory salute, visibly relieved and smiling.

What was your life like in jail? is a question that is asked of Binayak very often. The curiosity is natural, even more so because the person who spent two years in jail wasn't the stereotypical criminal. Binayak talks about the loss of human dignity, of human rights. About one particular fellow convict who became a close friend.

This was a young boy of perhaps twenty-four who had spent seven years in jail for murdering his father. Actually he had been forced to kill his drunk, abusive father in self-defence, and to prevent him from killing his mother. Once while talking to the students of a Mumbai college about this young boy facing possibly an entire life in jail, Binayak got extremely emotional, his voice choked up and he had to take a moment to recover his composure. He then went on to speak about how gentle and harmless that boy was, how he had almost no legal recourse, no money and therefore, in all probability, would rot in jail forever.

He talked of other prisoners, older ones, who hadn't seen their families in over fifteen years due to the small impediment of perhaps Rs 300-500, the cost of a bus ticket from the village back home to Raipur jail. Since many of them were illiterate and so too were their families, letters were of no use, phones an expensive option. So they would rely on relatively richer visitors from neighbouring villages to bring them fleeting news of their loved ones. One convict told Binayak he hadn't seen his son for over twelve years and probably wouldn't be able to recognize him today even if he did.

These stories have in a way stayed with Binayak, much after he has escaped the harshness of jail life. Beatings in jail are routine, he says; convicts caught in minor misdemeanours are beaten mercilessly, one man by fifteen strong, able-bodied *lambardars,* till the man falls down and is kicked unconscious.

The stereotypical images of "awful conditions in jail" including the unhygienic food, overcrowding, heat and dust and noise, bothered Binayak not one bit. What bothered him, what overshadowed everything else by far, was the stark fact that jail is a place where hope is totally extinguished for such large numbers of people in the country, and for such a long, long time, waiting for those wheels of justice to grind ever so slowly. Binayak says wryly that all jails should post a signboard outside, "Abandon hope, all ye who enter here".

For him, personally, hope was never extinguished because there was a full-fledged, active and articulate movement going on outside and inside jail. But for Ilina and the rest of the circle of family and friends, it was an endurance test, not just the inadequate meetings behind meshed barriers but having to hear police statements like "Don't worry, we won't break his legs", made and meant to intimidate and frighten them.

For too many months now, too much time spent in too many court rooms has cast a shadow over the lives of the Sen family. For them to be able to live without fear, with their heads held high, this trial *must* end soon.

Chapter Nine

THE CAMPAIGN FOR FREEDOM

Worldwide

23rd April 2008, Washington DC
In a letter addressed to the President and Prime Minister of India
and Chief Minister of Chhattisgarh, Dr Nils Dulaire, President of
the Global Health Council, (reaching out to140 countries across 6
continents) writes,
"It is not our intent to interfere with the judicial process. We simply
request that this doctor's good works and highly regarded reputation
as a man of science and service, serve as a guarantee of his obligation
to return to India to participate in a just and fair judicial process,
after the awards ceremony. The world is watching this case."

Binayak Sen was selected by an international jury of public health
professionals for the prestigious Jonathan Mann award for years of
service to poor and tribal communities in India, for establishing self-
sustaining health care services where none existed and for unwavering
commitment to civil liberties and human rights.

Binayak Sen is the first South Asian to be honoured by the Global
Health Council.

There are causes worth fighting for and there are people worth fighting for, even in today's age of jaded cynicism and indifference where public protest and candle light vigils have become routine, a part of people's righteous, spontaneous expression, but discarded as easily once the event and the media bytes are over.

But the rare combination of a good man fighting a good cause has the innate power to transform public inertia into a sustained mass movement, without a single word being said. Binayak Sen's selfless and consistent work did the talking and countless others did the work. Thus a campaign for freedom took root in the hearts and minds of supporters in different corners of the world, creating a unique solidarity, unknown and unmatched in scale in contemporary India. It came to be known as the Free Binayak Sen campaign, with volunteers scrambling to offer help in any way they could.

They came in huge numbers, spilling onto the streets of Raipur, Delhi, Mumbai, Kolkata, Chennai, Pune, Bangalore, Lucknow, London, San Francisco, New York city, Washington DC, Berlin, Paris...the list is endless...protesting, wearing cloth posters demanding the release of Binayak Sen, shouting slogans, singing songs, reciting poems, courting arrest, making fiery speeches, sitting on relay hunger fasts, holding medical camps, organizing film festivals in Binayak's name...

It took almost two years to the day of relentless work to keep up the pressure. First, to let the nation and the world know a good man was unjustly in jail, and then, to work towards getting him out of that jail. In the beginning, it was the inner circle of close friends that immediately swung into action. And as a support group, given that Binayak and Ilina had worked in the social development sector for more than twenty five years, it was both impressive and widespread. The network they belonged to,

PUCL activists, MFC members, the progressive intelligentsia of the country that they were connected with already, over decades of work with various NGOs, provided the crucial base for the groundswell of support.

That initial support had a snowballing effect and the campaign took on unique dimensions. The alumni, staff and students of CMC, Vellore held rallies, signed petitions, organized awareness campaigns about Binayak's work and incarceration, and officially and unofficially "pulled every string they could to get our person released." Dr Zachariah, one of Binayak's teachers says that CMC has perhaps never taken this kind of stand for any other alumnus as it did for Binayak. The entire campaign was run principally by the alumni association, but a lot of CMC connections were undoubtedly used as well, even if it was not in an organizational or institutional manner.

Along with Dr Zachariah, Dr Sara Bhattacharji and other alumni mobilized the CMC community to protest against Binayak's arrest almost immediately. She was one of the first to go to Raipur to meet the chief secretary as part of a group that included lawyers, JNU activists, Medico Friends Circle members, to hand over the signature petition and present their arguments. The encounter proved futile. The chief secretary heard them out because they were "a high-powered delegation and he had to humour them," according to Sara's information. Other CMC doctors, in their individual capacities, approached ministers and contacts at the highest level but drew a blank in the initial days after the arrest.

As for the all-important medical fraternity to which Binayak belonged, the response was mixed at best and shockingly apathetic at worst. Many doctors agreed that Binayak was a good man but "being associated with Naxalites was not a good thing and they wanted no part of it". The local Chhattisgarh doctors too were afraid that they would be targeted or marked by the state if they spoke up for their colleague. Dr Jacob John of CMC, Vellore who was President of the Paediatric Association tried hard to get them on board but says they backed out on the technicality that since Binayak was officially not a member, they could not help at all. Everybody was wary, everybody was running scared.

The Ganyari doctors were the only doctors in Chhattisgarh who tried to garner support in various ways, through meetings and press conferences, contributing to a book "Doctors in Support of Binayak Sen", providing moral support to the family and information about the case and Binayak to anyone in civil society who needed it, and most importantly, keeping his Bagrumnala clinic going in his absence despite being extremely hard-pressed for time.

The other twin pillars of support, apart from family and personal friends, were the PUCL and MFC, for whom Binayak was "one of their own." Rajendra Sail, Sudha Bhardwaj, Abhay Shukla, Anand Phadke, Manisha Gupte, Amar Jesani, Kavita Shrivastava, Satya Sivaraman, the Ganyari doctors...these were some of the main people who were Binayak's "own", the planners and executors of the different strategies to free Binayak Sen in the days and months before the campaign even acquired its name or identity.

The chorus of solidarity from the Nobel Laureates, national and international organizations, the academics, the physicians, and the celebrities undoubtedly added stature and credibility but the sustenance of the campaign depended on focused volunteer groups. The core group centred around the people Binayak had either worked with or served in his dual identity as a doctor and defender of human rights.

~

Sixty-six-year-old Rajendra Sail is a person you would like in your corner when in trouble. That quality actually holds true for all the core team members of the Free Binayak Sen campaign. They stood firm behind their man, immediately started drawing up action plans and strategies for the campaign, provided moral and sometimes physical support (in terms of actual presence) to the Sen family, and most importantly, never gave up!

Rajendra Sail is the long-haired President of the Chhattisgarh PUCL, a distinctive figure with a loud, resounding voice ideal for delivering impassioned speeches which he does, for Binayak, his colleague and friend of more than three decades, as well as for many others still imprisoned in jails in the state.

His most reassuring (visibly so) strength lies in calmly and efficiently dealing with any and as many obstacles thrust in one's path on any given day. I personally witnessed this on the second anniversary of Binayak's arrest, at a protest rally in May 2009. As the procession of peaceful, slogan-shouting protestors tried walking towards the Central Jail in Raipur, the police put up barricades and blocked the way. Immediately Rajendra Sail led the demonstrators towards Subhash Stadium, the regularly-used venue for courting mass arrest, which is what followed, in an equally peaceful yet effective manner. The more passionate and young student brigade of the rally had urged him to let them break the police barricades and brave the *lathis* in front of the jail, but to no avail.

After seeing to the legal formalities connected to the case, Rajendra Sail and the Chhattisgarh PUCL immediately organized the first rally of support on May 24, 2007 in Raipur. Fourteen people's organizations including political parties and social movements took part, registering an impressive attendance of over 350 people.

A much larger demonstration rally followed on May 28, says Sail, with the Chhattisgarh Mukti Morcha leading an alliance of "strong, left democratic forces". According to Sail, "Thousands of people, workers, peasants, women, youth, industrial-rural came for the rally. They had just one agenda—to protest against Binayak Sen's arrest and the draconian CSPSA Act."

Sail continues ticking off dates on his fingers, mentioning another all-India protest day on May 31 in Raipur, a convention on June 25, a midnight rally on August 15, the last 2007 protest on December 19, and a "lot of letter-writing and meeting the Governor in between."

And then he fast-forwards to June 2008, to the group fasts held in Raipur, spearheaded by Magsaysay award winner Dr Sandeep Pandey and CMM leader Prem Narayan Verma.

How did Binayak Sen fare in jail in the intervening months and why is it that his story remained largely untold for almost an entire year for the average Indian? Sail's explanation is fast and furious, "Regional media, the local media here in Raipur was very biased against Binayak. They would either report falsehoods or just not report anything at all. Often despite the number of people supporting our rallies, the local media would publish a photograph and write not a word! In press conferences, three or four newspapers out of fifteen would turn up. So regional reporting was unfavourable and national media never highlighted the issue. That turned out to be a major weakness for our cause."

Abhay Shukla, co-ordinator of SAATHI, a pro-people health advocacy team linked to CEHAT, and one of the key mobilizers of MFC's initiatives in the freedom campaign, agrees wholeheartedly about the partisan role of the local media in the early days. " We (MFC) held two press conferences in Raipur and Bilaspur in May and June 2007 and it was quite clear that the local media were demonizing him, not even calling him a doctor. They would call him the Naxals' courier, messenger, postman. We encountered a very hostile media," he says frankly.

Even as the MFC continued with its agenda, holding more press conferences in Chhattisgarh, publishing a twenty-page booklet, "Release Dr Binayak Sen", describing his work as a doctor, development and human rights activist, outlining the legal case and explaining the various ways that people could help, later bringing out a more detailed book, "Indian Doctor in Jail: Doctors in Defence of Binayak Sen", the people behind MFC's efforts, individually and as groups, also faced the heat of leading Binayak's freedom campaign. Both in and outside the state of Chhattisgarh. The Jan Swasthya Sahyog doctors at Ganyari, Bilaspur were in the direct line of state fire and ire but MFC colleagues in far-away Pune did not escape scrutiny either. In his small office in a nondescript building in Kothrud, Pune, the burly and bespectacled Abhay Shukla talks of subtle intimidation by the police as soon as he (along with his colleagues) started organizing the Binayak campaign. Questions were asked about what he did in Pune; all papers, documents, signature campaign details were demanded, the surveillance was on.

This is par for the course, according to Abhay. If you speak up for the poor and you do it consistently, take it to its logical conclusions, then you are definitely going to face the wrath of the state. As long as an NGO provides training and distributes medicines in a village it is acceptable but the minute it starts asking serious and uncomfortable questions about corruption or why services are not reaching the people, it comes under the radar, the way that Binayak did. Thus, he (Abhay) emphasizes the need for developing strategies for health activists and professionals so that tomorrow if more Binayak Sens, less well connected to PUCL or MFC groups, are faced with similar situations, at least there will be a large number of people who will stand up for them. Because not everyone has a PUCL or a CMC or an MFC standing tall behind them.

And Binayak's story, played out yesterday in Bastar and other parts of Chhattisgarh can tomorrow be Abhay's story in Pune and other parts of Maharashtra. Or the Ganyari doctors' story in Bilaspur. Or the story of unknown people in unknown regions facing similar situations and responding to them the Binayak way. After all, the issues are so similar—collaborative health care initiatives involving training community health workers, especially women, establishing First Contact Care for common ailments like diarrhoea, common cold, cough, anaemia, malaria, tuberculosis, etc. then progressing to asking deeper, meaningful questions about the politics of health.

Abhay, who was part of a medical team that visited Dantewada district in July 2007 to investigate "what led to Binayak's arrest", shares his insights. He describes a chilling and total blockade of health services to almost 500-600 villages in the district on account of their being considered 'Maoist'. These people were left to fend for themselves. Binayak had written about this in his report, says Abhay, and this was why his voice was silenced by the government. "As an articulate, upper middle class physician working with human rights at the national level, having linkages with the PUCL and other national bodies, Binayak was in the forefront. The government knew that if they can silence Binayak, they can silence most of the others who are in the middle ground, basically they can shut down the democratic space, so that any form of military offensive like the Salwa Judum can go on and on without anyone pointing out what is actually happening,"

Manisha Gupte, MFC member and another fearless "Binayak Sen", minces no words while analyzing the MFC and its support to the campaign. Speaking to her helps demystify for me the MFC which until then I had imagined to be a conglomerate of intensely serious, extremely intellectual doctors who discussed various ailments plaguing the health care system of this country. Not really, says Manisha, who is the vivacious and energetic founding trustee of MASUM, a development group with a strongly feminist perspective and a democratic approach. MFC doesn't only comprise the medical fraternity, she tells me, despite the name. Today almost sixty per cent of its members are not doctors. They are also not, as often labelled by critics, disillusioned with medicine, but a group of thinking, critical and articulate people who don't understand medicine as just a doctor's business, but as everybody's business. Health is about mind, body and a sense of peace and well being with your micro and macro environment. "Take the swine flu panic in Pune for example. If I go and distribute masks to people I am called a philanthropist but if I ask about the politics of Tamiflu (the tablet to cure it), then I am a 'Binayak Sen'! That is where MFC stands, you cannot go around only distributing medicines when the causes of ill-health are based on the social determinants of health—food, water, land, right to education, right to safety," she continues her detailed analysis.

Asking questions about why there is illness, why we still have malnourishment despite never having a shortage of food since 1964, questioning disparity, discrimination, violence—both overt and structural violence—this is where one is labelled dangerous, whether it is MFC or *any* person with a conscience. "Those who are courageous and seen too often at problematic intersections in particular places, like Binayak, bear the brunt while we in Maharashtra are relatively safe. But ultimately I think Binayak's case was like a steaming hot morsel that the government had put in its mouth, too hot to swallow, too hot to spit out...he got all the focus. People who had never ever heard of the Salwa Judum have now heard of it. International support poured in and he appealed to the common mind, so ordinary people supported him as well. If someone is urban and educated, he is automatically elite and if he chooses to take a tough path, it impresses people," she says, reinforcing my own impressions for the many reasons of the support received during the campaign. Support that extended way beyond India's borders.

On May 16 and 24, 2007, Amnesty International issued statements of protest urging the Chhattisgarh government to end the harassment of human rights defenders like Binayak and others in the state. Noam Chomsky and other prominent intellectuals followed suit on June 16, claiming that Binayak's arrest was an attempt to intimidate democratic voices speaking out against human rights violations in the state. The British House of Commons published an Early Day Motion on June 7, 2007 in Binayak's support, with several British MPs cutting across party lines, joining in. The British Medical Journal published an article on June 9, reporting both the arrest and a protest outside the Indian High Commission in London. "The Wall Street Journal" of November 12, 2007 carried an article entitled, "Indian unrest ensnares a doctor: rights activists such as Dr Sen caught in the middle". The paper also carried a follow-up letter four days later: "Good works, bad reward".

The Indian members of parliament maintained a studied silence and indifferent stand on the Binayak Sen issue that same year. And as far as the Indian national press was concerned, not a single newspaper or magazine covered the Binayak Sen story till he had spent almost a whole year in jail. "Tehelka" was perhaps the only exception, highlighting the issue right from the beginning, at the time of the arrest in 2007, then again in a more detailed account of Binayak's work and plight in jail in February 2008, with follow-up stories in May, June, right up to his release on bail and later. The only other media coverage (apart from news reports based on mere press releases) was on "Infochange" a popular news and development features website, which published an article by Sandhya Srinivasan in May 2007 in which she wrote, "Middle class Indians feel no sympathy for people like Binayak Sen (and Arun Ferreira)". She was to be proved wrong a year later once the campaign and public pressure gathered momentum and press coverage.

Unique ways of support however continued for Binayak Sen. CMC, Vellore and the Centre for Social Medicine and Community Health at JNU (of which Binayak was once a faculty member) came up with the novel concept of holding free medical clinics and camps for the poor, as a tribute to Binayak's work and as a way to also peacefully campaign for his release. The JNU students union held the first such camp in March 2008 for 250 daily contract labourers on the university campus. Others joined in, all over the country—Coimbatore, Bangalore, Kolkata, Bhopal, Trivandrum—spreading awareness about Binayak's case simultaneously.

In April 2008 when Binayak's trial finally began, there was still no mention of the case in the national media. It was left to Human Rights Watch to issue a statement questioning the possibility of Binayak being given a fair trial, considering that the presiding judge allowed only one of Binayak's supporters to attend the hearings at a time, despite provisions in international law that trials be made public. Brad Adams, Asia director of Human Rights Watch even suggested the venue be moved to another state to ensure fairness. This of course was not possible but right until the first anniversary of Binayak being in jail, the only people protesting were principally those in the loop—family, friends and activists, in India and abroad.

The anniversary changed all of that—the scale of support increased a hundred-fold and it grabbed the attention of the media, finally. A coordinated, concerted campaign began, in full swing, both online and on the ground. "Free Binayak Sen" film festivals were held at Jantar Mantar, New Delhi, in Trivandrum, Bangalore, Chennai, Shimoga, Gorakhpur, Imphal, Mumbai, Pune, on themes varying from human rights to nutrition to environmental pollution. Even in far-off Jalpaiguri, small groups of people attended six-hour long film festivals organized by Prabir Chatterjee on issues that Binayak is involved with. In one of the films, "Development Flows", by Bijju Toppo and Meghnath, there is even a short clip of Binayak himself, examining the x-ray of a displaced villager in Chhattisgarh. Binayak posters and leaflets in Bengali were also distributed at this festival. This is just one more example of the kind of reach and response of different forms of advocacy used in the campaign.

The conventional routes were taken too, of course, necessary for any such movement. Protest marches ranged from candle light vigils in Bangalore, conventions in Kolkata, demonstrations in Chennai, including a rather quaint one by children performing "parai" or voice of the oppressed, cultural artists evenings in New Delhi with celebrities like Arundhati Roy and others attending in a show of solidarity, to slogan-shouting outside the Indian consulate in New York, San Francisco, London, Scottish campaigners in Edinburgh. The arc of both the nature and volume of support seemed astonishing to people reading about it for the first time, not even knowing who Binayak Sen was, in the first instance.

The crowning glory was the appeal by twenty-two Nobel Laureates from around the world, writing to India's President, Prime Minister and Chhattisgarh state authorities that Binayak should be allowed to travel to the US to receive the Jonathan Mann award conferred on him in May 2008, also expressing grave concern that he was "being incarcerated solely for peacefully exercising his fundamental rights."

Long curious as to how this enormously impressive task was facilitated, I asked Ilina how twenty-two Nobel Laureates were persuaded to sign this letter of support. The answer was startlingly simple. It was routed through some of CMC's extremely distinguished alumni, reputed scientists and physicians themselves.

The same applied to the Early Day Motions introduced in the House of Commons in the UK. The CMC alumni network and the bonding was powerful and potent.

Back in Raipur, the Chhattisgarh unit of the PUCL and various people's organizations observed a day-long *dharna* on the first anniversary at Budha Talab, by then the fixed venue for such functions. It was attended by 450 workers, peasants, political party workers and intellectuals. They drew up a plan for taking forward their agenda, beyond agitating for Binayak's release to stopping the state war against its own citizens, banning the Salwa Judum and repealing the Black Law (CSPSA). They chose the time-honoured weapon of a chain-hunger strike or fasting for ten days, from June 16 to 25, 2008.

More than seventy organizations joined in with the fasts that began in Raipur, not just in India but in the US, UK, Sri Lanka, Nepal, Bangladesh, Thailand, Australia and the UAE, offering support both literally and morally.

Rajendra Sail says, "There were at least 250 people at the *pandal* every day and yet the government remained indifferent. Instead of making the requisite arrangements for drinking water or medical check-up facilities, as is the norm everywhere for fasting protestors, the local authorities (Raipur Municipal Corporation) actually dumped garbage near the protestors!"

While the DGP Chhattisgarh, Vishwaranjan, wrote a scathing and sarcastic article against the fasting activists titled "Gandhi, escape from the midst of pseudo-Gandhians" in the Hindi daily "Hari Bhoomi", published locally in Raipur, the press by and large did not report the fasts, despite the presence of a Magsaysay award winner Sandeep Pandey, and activists from the National Alliance of People's Movement, or NAPM.

Media coverage until then had mainly been restricted to articles in "Tehelka" and "Outlook", editorials in "The Hindu", an online article by the BBC and another in the South China Morning Post. The Indian Express carried a three-part series and an editorial on Binayak but only in January 2009.

The denial of bail to Binayak from the High Court (in the state) and the Supreme Court in December 2008, evoked sharp criticism and what the PUCL termed a hugely successful rally of protest, but since the media did not report it with any seriousness, most people did not know that 2008 had also gone by with the good doctor still languishing in jail. Television channels too had not yet found Binayak Sen to be "byte worthy". That would come later.

The most remarkable and lasting effort in 2008, apart from the group fasts, was the unique online activism—the Facebook Free Binayak Sen campaign that is very much around even today with 2132 members and its own website, binayaksen.net.

Kamayani Bali Mahabal is the feisty, no-holds-barred, fiercely dedicated face behind this advocacy group, Anivar Aravind and Sukla Sen being the other executors of this modern tool of mass, in-a-second, in-your-face, pledge your support, fight for your cause, on the Internet.

Kamayani is a short, slim, trendily-dressed fireball of energy who you just cannot say NO to. Whether she is urging people to sign petitions online to free Binayak Sen or buy the specially designed black T-shirts with his smiling picture imprinted on it, or asking for entries of poems for the 2009 Binayak calendar, she is indefatigable. And so un-selfconscious about it that you capitulate instantly and do what she wants you to do in her crusade to right the wrongs in the world. Binayak is one of many causes and battles she believes need to be fought and won. A trained clinical psychologist, journalist, lawyer, human rights activist, she is also the founder of a human rights organization called AHSAAS that helped victims of Punjab terrorism with legal remedies.

I ask her about the Facebook campaign for Binayak Sen. She answers animatedly, speaking in rapid-fire tones, alternating expressions chasing her mobile face, "We thought not many people know about Binayak, a doctor behind bars. I myself got to know a year after he was in jail. The advantage with online activism, the reason it is used so much, is that within a second, it is all over the world. It is important for our advocacy initiatives and for telling people about human rights violations."

Kamayani never ever imagined they would receive the kind of response they did, either in the kinds of people who logged in or in the sheer number of outraged, sympathetic, moved, awed and inspired Facebook users who wanted to help, in any way they could. Even those who did not join the 2132-member group wanted to know more about Binayak, about what the Salwa Judum was and why the Supreme Court could release Varun Gandhi on bail while denying the same to Binayak!

Kamayani posted (and continues to post even today) information related to each and every protest, rally, petition, cultural evening, lecture, song, poem, article, film festival, medical camp, held in support of Binayak Sen and related issues as well, on human rights and social justice. The Free Binayak Sen campaign proved especially providential when it came to the weekly reportage of the Raipur rallies that proved to be the piece de resistance of the freedom campaign. Week after week, as people peacefully fasted in Raipur, the Free Binayak Sen campaign faithfully posted their status on Facebook for the world to read and react.

Binayak too credits the Raipur rallies for turning the tide in his favour. From March 16 to May 14, 2009 the participants would have done even Gandhi proud, so firm was their goal, so fierce their dedication.

In fact, it *was* a mass civil disobedience movement very much on the lines of those propagated by Mahatma Gandhi and Martin Luther King, with batches of 50-100 people courting arrest, Monday after Monday, in front of Central Jail, Raipur where Binayak was imprisoned.

The first week's rally was flagged off with 59 protestors from 7 states courting arrest, with Magsaysay award-winner Sandeep Pandey and documentary film maker Anand Patwardhan among those demanding the release of Binayak Sen.

The next Monday, Anusuya Sen, Binayak's eighty-three-year-old mother, led the rally, singing an inspirational Bengali song, *"Aami Bhoy Korbo na"* (We are not afraid). Activist Satinath Sarangi and 50 survivors of the Bhopal gas tragedy joined in, people who know the meaning of injustice and keep fighting to end it wherever they witness it.

Week 3 saw solidarity protests in other parts of the country as well. Kamayani and a motley team of activists that included lawyers, teachers, doctors and feminists wore their Free Binayak T-shirts (sponsored by a Facebook donor and sold as well, as part of the campaign) and picked one railway station in Mumbai each Monday—gathering as many people as possible to distribute flyers, collect signatures, and mobilize Mumbaikars. That particular Monday they got 100 Mumbaikars to sign, no mean achievement.

The fourth batch of 104 protestors, mainly activist groups, also held a press conference in Raipur which was addressed, among others, by Arundhati Roy and Abhay Shukla, who apart from being a prominent MFC member, also led the "Pune Solidarity Committee for the Release of Dr Sen".

In her inimitable style, Arundhati Roy minced no words:

"That Dr Sen should continue to be in prison when the case against him has almost completely fallen through says a great deal about the very grave situation in Chhattisgarh today. There is a civil war in this state. Hundreds are being killed and imprisoned. Hundreds of thousands of the poorest of the poor are hiding in the forests, fearing for their lives. They have no access to food, to markets, to schools or healthcare. The thousands who have been moved into the camps of the government-backed people's militia, the Salwa Judum, are also trapped in sordid encampments, which have to be guarded by armed police. Hatred, violence and brutality are being cynically spread, pitting the poor against the poorest.

There is very little doubt that Dr Sen is in prison because he spoke out against this policy of the state government, because he opposed the formation of the Salwa Judum. His incarceration is meant to silence dissent, and criminalize democratic space. It is meant to create a wall of silence around the civil war in Chhattisgarh. It is meant to absorb all our attention so that the stories of the hundreds of other nameless, faceless people—those without lawyers, without the attention of journalists—who are starving and dying in the forests, go unnoticed and unrecorded.

Dr Binayak Sen spent the best part of his life working among the poorest people in India, who live far away from the government's attentions, with no access to clinics, hospitals, doctors or medicines. He has saved thousands from certain death from malaria, diarrhoea, and other easily treatable illnesses. And yet, he is the one in jail, while those who boast openly about mass murder are free to go about their business, and even stand for elections. What does this say about us? About who we are and where we're going?"

Equally articulate and possibly provocative speeches and slogans were raised, intentionally so, by Medha Patkar, the fiery leader of the Narbada Bachao Andolan and National Alliance of People's

Movement who led the eighth week of the Raipur rally on May 4, with 200 protestors. She stormed her way, courting arrest, with these words, "Give Binayak Sen bail or else give us jail. We are prepared to go to jail and stay with Binayak, we share his values. Why should the Chhattisgarh government not show courage and put us in jail with him as well?"

The continued, majority presence of many local activists from Chhattisgarh like VCA's Himanshu Kumar, displaced villagers and many, many ordinary workers gave lie to the local media reports that only the elite supported Binayak Sen, a claim scornfully dismissed by Sudha Bhardwaj who was a staunch participant from the beginning. "Every week's rally saw peasants from Raigarh, contract workers from Bhilai and Raipur, survivors of the Bhopal gas tragedy, people from Bagrumnala…these are all voiceless people. On the one hand, the media never represents their voice, on the other, if a Medha Patkar or an Arundhati Roy does voice their concern or Binayak's, then you say this is an elite person?" concludes Sudha.

Binayak concurs wholeheartedly. "The Raipur rally was central to the whole campaign and it was led by people who were the backbone of the CMM. Their current situation is very difficult and yet they did that work, without which the rally would not have taken place. The Bagrumnala people also participated in whole measure. Elite people who supported me got more publicity, they get reported, that's natural. People like Medha, Arundhati are people who represent large forces; some beauty queen is not coming to support me!"

Others among the so-called "elite" roll call were Nobel laureate Amartya Sen, poet Mahashweta Devi, historian Romila Thapar, intellectuals like Irfan Habib and Dr Ashok Mitra, sociologist Jean Dreze, film makers Shyam Benegal and Sudhir Mishra and many more, all of whom signed petitions urging the government to "Drop the charges NOW".

All over the world, echoes of the same refrain were heard, whether it was a group of Scottish doctors chaining themselves together in Edinburgh, signifying protest, or an e-petition in England or the Committee of Concerned Scientists (CCS) writing to the government to release Binayak.

As the year 2009 slipped into the month of May and the day of the second anniversary of Binayak in jail drew closer, the scale and fervour of all the activities, online and on the ground, stepped up in geometric proportions.

"Two years too much", was the slogan everyone adopted while completing their assigned tasks in the freedom campaign. And thus, Round Two of the freedom campaign began, with double the vigour. Everyone gave it their very best shot, appalled that two whole years had gone by with Binayak behind bars.

In a clear and vivid memory of my very first exposure to what I later learnt was the finale of the Free Binayak Sen campaign—the massive rally and courting of arrest on May 14, 2009 in Raipur—as I walked among the 600-odd, slogan-shouting protestors, their voices reaching a crescendo near destination end at Subhash Stadium, not too far from Central Jail, I recall wondering if the sounds of support could be heard by the man inside.

"Dr Binayak Sen ko riha karo, riha karo, riha karo. Kale kanoon radd karo," I can still hear the crowds chanting that day. Was Binayak aware of the extent of the activities launched worldwide on his behalf? Of course he was, he says, and the only reason that hope was not extinguished for him in jail was because there was an entire movement outside working to free him. Cultural evenings with singers, poets, theatre artistes, protest paintings, recitations, film festivals, candlelight processions, signature

campaign, student *dharnas,* medical camps, poster campaigns, cycle rallies and pamphleteering, public seminars marked the day in New Delhi, Raipur, Mumbai, Pune, Andhra Pradesh, Jharkhand, Kerala, Karnataka, Tamil Nadu, West Bengal, Gujarat and Rajasthan.

Abroad, the solidarity was no less widespread, with demonstrations outside the London High Commission, a vigil in Bristol's city centre, candlelight vigils, human rights film festivals and day-long hunger fasts in various parts of the United States, Germany, Japan, Sweden, France, Canada...

On May 25, 2009 when the Supreme Court granted him bail unconditionally in sixty seconds, the celebration was equally shared and heartfelt across telephone lines, emails, Facebook accounts, and in person.

Kamayani, who had been getting ready to go for a demonstration since it was a Monday, distributed *mithai* to people instead.

So did Rajendra Sail at the Chattisgarh PUCL office in Raipur. The Free Binayak Sen campaign had cost the PUCL Rs 5 lakh, countless volunteers and almost two years, but their general-secretary was home free that day.

~

In the end, Ilina Sen went to Washington DC on May 29, 2008, to collect the Jonathan Mann award on her husband's behalf, along with their daughters Pranhita and Aparajita. All the lobbying in the world, quite literally, did not allow Binayak to collect his award in person. In her acceptance speech on Binayak's behalf, Ilina echoed Binayak's views on health and human rights, reiterating, like Jonathan Mann, that unless you try to change the world, it will never change!

Chapter Ten

JOURNEY'S END

Wardha

" No, I absolutely cannot do this, I'm sorry. It would not be right on my part, nor would it be correct to show something which is not true," says Binayak firmly, shaking his head for extra emphasis.

He watches my dismayed face and listens to my lengthy explanations patiently but remains unmoved. Nothing I can say, none of my pleas shake his resolve and twenty minutes later, silence envelops us as I realize just how firm and uncompromising he can be.

The impasse is to do with my request that he "go for a round", examine patients at the Shaheed Hospital so as to provide the requisite visuals for the documentary film that I am making on him.

Binayak objects to doing this because Saibal Jana is the doctor in charge at Shaheed Hospital, so he feels *he* should be filmed performing these tasks. All of my arguments, that Binayak himself used to visit Shaheed to see patients once a week till the end of 2006, that Saibal will be filmed as well, that I need a lot of visuals of Binayak since he is the principal focus of the film, cut no ice whatsoever.

Eventually we resolve the issue by Binayak agreeing to reminisce about his years at Shaheed, standing *outside* the hospital and since he's a paediatrician, to be filmed with lots of children, hopefully making up for the lack of visuals in this manner. It seems like such a small issue to me, but the lines of right and wrong are clearly demarcated for Binayak, and he will *not* do something he believes is incorrect. At that moment it is hard to tell whether I am more irritated or admiring of such an attitude; acceptance finally wins the day and we move on to discuss far more troubling issues in his equally troubled state of Chhattisgarh.

It is March 1, 2010, the festive day of Holi, and we are in the comfortable and tastefully decorated living room of Ilina's home in Wardha. She is the head of the Women's Studies Department at the Mahatma Gandhi University and commutes between this home and A-26, Surya Apartments in Raipur. Ilina has left for her lectures, Pranhita has finished feeding her new puppies, Billo has returned to Mumbai to resume college after the Holi break, it's just Binayak and I over the next few hours, completing unfinished discussions of the previous day and "unsatisfactory telephone conversations" of the previous week.

Binayak is not much of a telephone person. After initial pleasantries are exchanged, and if any problematic topic comes up thereafter, he immediately hands over the phone to Ilina, abdicating responsibility. *She* then irons out the difficulty, offers suggestions and solutions, takes charge. It is a role she slips into effortlessly, as her daughters have informed me on several occasions.

The days before this meeting had been rather upsetting. My

film shoot had to be postponed at the last minute because the police had threatened the villagers of Bagrumnala where we were going to film Binayak re-starting his Friday clinics. Consequently Prahladji, Rupantar's manager and our main contact person on the ground who went to Bagrumnala in advance to set things up for us, warned us to keep away for the time being. The villagers were afraid to show up, he said to me, and the police would be there in full force, watching us shoot. So would the "other side", and he could no longer take the onus of responsibility for our safety or that of our expensive camera equipment. He ended with a statement that silenced me at the other end of the phone, *"Doc Saab jab bhi yahan aate hain poori fauj (police) peeche-peeche aati hai* (whenever he comes here, the entire police force follows him)."

Ilina corroborated this shocking statement that night. "This is why Binayak has stopped going to Bagrumnala, he doesn't want to inconvenience the villagers…once he leaves the village, the police go to the villagers and harass them, asking them about his visit." She too advised caution and the shoot was duly postponed.

The next morning Binayak spoke out emotionally across an unclear telephone line, "Can you imagine what it feels like not to be able to go back to my own clinic? These are very hard times we are facing, difficult circumstances in our state. Come to Wardha, let us talk it over."

It is five months since I met him during his trial in Raipur in September 2009 and more than seven since our first meeting in July. In the intervening months, I have also met him in Vellore, in Mumbai apart from meeting and interviewing his friends and colleagues all over the country—in Delhi, Mumbai, Pune, Vellore, Ganyari, Bilaspur, Dalli Rajhara, Dhamtari, Bagrumnala, Dantewada.

In a very real sense therefore, this is journey's end for me, a farewell visit, barring my film shoot later. Inevitable then, the retrospective assessment, the comparisons of meetings first and last, the personality analysis, howsoever ephemeral and superficial they may appear to those who know Binayak Sen closely and for long.

Mine *is* after all, an outsider's point of view, never mind that my first waking thought every day for over seven months has been related to Binayak Sen. Several meetings, discussions, telephone conversations or email exchanges still do not alter the fact that I remain the quintessential outsider, looking in. Friendly but always formal, asking permission. To take a look into their lives, into the past, into a world that is unfamiliar to most people and yes, as Binayak told me at the very beginning, I now see for myself that it *is* a privileged world.

Shared and enjoyed only by those who *lived* it, experienced its incredible highs and lows, displayed the necessary staying power and resilience, coped with a common past. It is a world that does not admit outsiders—at best, they can admire it from a distance. To gain admittance to that world you have to have paid your dues and *then* you speak the same language. I flashback into the first time I realized this fact, when it literally stared me in the face, in the faces of twenty-four remarkable people.

The occasion is a PUCL meeting at their Raipur office in September 2009, the first after their General Secretary, Binayak was released from jail. No less than seventeen different organizations—NGOs and trade unions—gather together in what they call a *Jan Sanghatana,* their very own special characteristic and by their own definition, "the need of the hour". A broad-based alliance of democratic and secular forces, people's organizations with a common agenda, joined together on a platform provided by the PUCL. The medium-sized room has a circle of chairs, red curtains fluttering in the breeze, a "No Smoking" sign sharing space with old files and folders stacked on a steel cupboard. The small kitchen adjoining this room provides the welcome tea and biscuits served to everyone during the marathon four and a half hour discussion that follows. Democratically and expectedly, each and every speaker is given time to express his or her views and share his or her stories.

Most people have tales of struggle to narrate, of how battles are being fought, of social issues, of problems of the poor and most importantly, of how they *all* try to draw strength from the collective. Binayak has stressed this aspect repeatedly to me over the last seven months. Most speakers are fiery, articulate and passionate too, finding resonances among those listening to them here, several offer support and suggestions later. Binayak is the obvious centre of attraction, but only in the beginning, when PUCL President Rajendra Sail welcomes him back in their midst with the cryptic, half-humorous statement that even though he is out of jail, "Life itself is a jail".

Binayak offers personal thanks to everyone for their support and speaks briefly about the crisis situation especially in the field of human rights and especially in Chhattisgarh and how PUCL can address such issues, while also correcting shortcomings. He then retreats into relative anonymity, sitting quietly, taking notes, reading, taking a break occasionally to walk outside and greet the many people who hail him with delight but for the most part, he sits silently, a keen observer of the proceedings rather than an active participant.

The discussion—all four and a half hours of it—offers insights into the psyche of the "collective" that Binayak refers to constantly. These are committed people, lawyers, trade unionists, social workers, even a film maker, Ajay T G (arrested in 2008 and jailed for five months for alleged links with Naxals). The issues they are discussing are in the larger public interest, they themselves have nothing to gain and everything to lose by their continued involvement with volatile issues that are confrontational with the state.

They have all just witnessed the outcome of such an encounter, and yet they continue to form action plans for the future, undeterred. In fact, a member of the Chandarnagar Gram Sabha goes one step further. His reading of the fall-out of Binayak's arrest is radically different. "Since Binayak was arrested, people who were revolutionaries and attackers were forced into defensive mode—that was a tragedy. If we are truly *andolan-kari, sangharshi*, we should attack and wage a war against all corporates displacing tribals and *they* should be in defensive mode. We should also use the media in all this," he concludes.

Film maker Ajay TG says that the national visual media should be invited, the state media will not help, people concerned about Bastar should go to the area and live in the villages, week after week, the way the Raipur rallies were conducted for Binayak's release.

The man from Bastar, white kurta-pyjama clad Himanshu Kumar has travelled ten hours from Dantewada by bus to attend this meeting and expresses his views forcefully, "Very few people go to Dantewada (this was before the killing of seventy-six CRPF personnel in Dantewada when lots of people *did* go to Dantewada!), people don't cross the Indravati river for fear of getting shot, adivasis who take up arms in the face of torture and rape by policemen are labelled Maoists...those who are fighting are those who are in maximum pain, we are only supporting the hungry, we are well-fed, are we not? Injustice increases violence, justice and peace go hand in hand..." His words echo Binayak's statements, made to me, to others, to the media, over the last few months.

Himanshu also reaffirms the belief that much more needs to be done, that no real struggle is taking place today against the rich-poor divide of which the Salwa Judum is such an integral part. "We have become reactionary people, our revolutionary-ness is not being recognized, we need to re-establish our image or the state will destroy us. *Nizam badalne nahi wale,*" he wags his hands admonishingly.

Sudha Bhardwaj agrees with the need to think of a campaign to get people to come home, not just in Bastar but in other displaced areas as well. Violence automatically decreases as people are rehabilitated, with *gram sabhas*, jobs, development, she adds.

The debate continues over the future role and scope of the PUCL. Some dissenting voices feel it cannot fulfill the larger role, the revolutionary role, others feel it is the Big Brother to NGOs in the state, and its achievements, including Binayak's release and his subsequent nation-wide recognition, should not be minimized.

Rashmi Dwivedi, one of the only four women among twenty-three men in the gathering, wants the fight to be better fought, with the PUCL overcoming the weaknesses that made it possible for Binayak to be arrested in the first place.

Since there are as many as eight lawyers present in the room, suggestions are made that the PUCL plan an active task force for a legal strategy to get all the other cases under the CSPSA withdrawn as well, not just Binayak's case. Rajendra Sail confirms that 250 social activists are in jail under article 307. No one has bothered to write about them or campaign for their freedom.

Sadiq Ali warns of the danger to all human rights activists, especially lawyers fighting cases under the CSPSA. He compares Binayak to a thermometer, a test case. Sudha adds to this, saying that lawyers arguing cases under this Act are now being photographed as well, in a bid to intimidate them.

A young worker, Basant Sahu, robustly provides words of

encouragement, his tone is almost crusading, "Wherever there is *daman* (oppression) and *goli* (bullets), the PUCL reaches out, be it Kashmir, the North-East, anywhere...we need to decide how to fight."

Another pyjama-clad worker from the CMM, Rajnandgaon, says they should fight this in a historic manner and recalls the Naxalbari movement of 1968. His knowledge of the subject is impressive, it easily equals any of the political science lectures of my college days in Pune University.

Gautam Bandhopadhyay reiterates the fact that they only need to decide what to do, not that they have to do it, since the space that is left for human rights activists today is limited and if that too is not utilized properly, excesses will only increase drastically. His words prove prophetic six months later when the Unlawful Activities Prevention Act is clamped on activists nationwide.

Listening and watching these people speak passionately, stand up for causes and people they believe in, empathize with problems of the marginalized and unrepresented sections of society and follow up that empathy with deeds, not mere words, makes me feel humbled and inadequate, all at once.

You do what you have to do, what you are *meant* to do...the thought rebounds in my mind but at that particular moment it brings no comfort. I *still* feel guilty for not doing any of what I see people who also hold down regular jobs, committing to doing in front of me. And even though the issues they raise are serious and compelling, even dangerous, the camaraderie is strong, the shared laughter infectious. "We are all together so we are laughing after a long time," says Sudha and everyone agrees smilingly.

Binayak ends the meeting with familiar words, saying that almost all issues are linked to the one common one of displacement. All other issues are procedural issues, PUCL's role will be defined by what it does, its inherent nature is not to stand alone but to be with all, a concerned citizens' group, which takes up the central issue of displacement and violence. If one can reverse displacement, violence will automatically be lessened.

I recall Binayak speaking of these issues for the first time at our first meeting in July 2009, the content and thrust of the conversation was very much in the same vein. It was late at night, he was tired, yet impassioned in speech, choosing his words carefully, and I was learning things about Chhattisgarh and Binayak that I could never have learnt as effectively any other way: an analysis based on almost three decades of hands-on experience...

...that poverty is not a default option, that the situation is one where an extremely unjust regime is being maintained in place by structural violence of massive proportions.

...that there is an urgent need to reject military confrontation, military activity as a way of solving social problems, irrespective of *who* is perpetuating the violence, and certainly the major perpetrators are the forces associated with the state.

...that illegally declaring large areas of forests as state property, excluding people from those areas, branding those that resist as Maoists and killing them is undemocratic and should be brought to light before civil society in the country.

...that *somebody* has to oppose people in power who use terms like "sanitizing" or "cleansing" to kill human beings to solve a problem the way the Sri Lankan government did the Tamil problem.

...that if Mahatma Gandhi being the Father of the Nation has to have any meaning at all, then this kind of military adventurism on the part of the state has to be given up.

...that peace is not just the negation of violence but a basis for justice.

...that society itself should question the legitimacy of military confrontation, that the alternative of political engagement needs to be reinforced for a resolution of conflict.

Those would be the milestones, I remember him saying, that would be the way forward to try to mitigate the enormous suffering people were going through.

I don't think Binayak himself could have realized how prophetic his words would sound in the months to come or whether his formula of peace with justice and equity would be heard at all by people polarized into adopting hardened stances, aggressive posturing and dangerous paths.

But in each of the interviews he gave me, in each press statement, in every television interview, especially immediately after his release from prison when the electronic media too, gave him his fifteen minutes of fame, at every public forum, Binayak has been calling for peace with justice, not the peace of the graveyard, but a peace with equity for all, with the cessation of violence.

Right from that first meeting in his Surya Apartments home in Raipur to the last one in Wardha, over a span of seven eventful months, the one thing that remained constant and unwavering was Binayak's stand on what he believed in. *That* did not change at all. Everything else around him changed irrevocably.

The man who had talked wistfully of how attractive the idea of a normal life with family and friends appeared to him, slowly had to alter that definition of normalcy.

At first he still spoke of resuming his medical work and re-starting the Bagrumnala clinic. Villagers and health workers were eagerly awaiting his return, I had told him after my visit to his clinic, for them no one else would do. Though this was contrary to the system of health care that he has built up in the area, where community health workers are trained to cope with the medical needs of the villagers, Binayak acknowledged the compliments and tributes with a modest smile and said he would be joining them soon.

But this did not happen.

In an unforeseen turn of events, when Binayak and Ilina went to Vellore in August 2009 to get Binayak's heart condition treated by the CMC doctors, Ilina, diagnosed with breast cancer, had to have an immediate mastectomy, followed by six cycles of chemotherapy, also at CMC Vellore. That effectively chalked out the calendar for the Sens for the next five months or so. Binayak would not leave Ilina alone. Pranhita would replace him whenever he had to tour for a lecture, all of them commuting from Raipur to Vellore to Wardha. Sometimes, not often, trial exemptions were sought and granted on compassionate grounds but the strain and worry that the entire family went through can only be imagined at best.

Ilina summarized plans for the future in an earlier meeting in Vellore ruefully. "Lots of friends are suggesting Binayak should re-locate or take this fight to the national level. This was not part of our original calculation, that we would ever move out, it's unsettling, change is unsettling. And there has been too much change."

Normalcy for her was the life they led before the spectre of Salwa Judum or the state of Chhattisgarh stepped in, when they were involved with grassroots activism and people's problems but also happy and fulfilled. In fact interviews with the many different kinds of people who shared different periods of their lives with Binayak over thirty years, reinforced again and again what he had expressed at his very first meeting with me, the principle he chose to live his life by, conviviality. Whether they were friends or co-workers or people who he had trained, patients and doctors, everyone highlighted this particular aspect of Binayak's personality—that he went out of his way to help people, a lot of people. Not surprising therefore that he should be remembered with affection, with gratitude, with nostalgia for a time gone by.

Often times, the stories told were so fascinating you wished you had been a part of them, lived that life, shared those friends. In the journey to trace the life of Binayak Sen, I had in fact found so many Binayak Sens—committed, selfless, dedicated professionals who refused any personal credit for their efforts. People who were part of history, creating it, privileged to have lived it. I found it all fascinating, a world apart.

This was the rich, varied, satisfying life of the Sens till things started going terribly wrong in the state they lived in, the state that had recognized their work in the public health sphere, the state that had included them in their official committees.

~

Three months after his release from jail, at that same August Vellore meeting with the Sens, Binayak is still hopeful of his peace agenda, believing that people will join him, realizing that silence is not an alternative, that if one has to accept wholeheartedly the idea of citizenship then people have to participate in politics, making it ultimately something people create for themselves.

I am skeptical but he insists that more and more people will be drawn into larger fields of duty, of involvement at least, that without this, society will not be a good place to live in. "We cannot be depending only on the police to maintain peace, that's for sure," he argues vehemently.

And *that* is something that needs to be made clear to everybody, especially the ordinary people, the middle class that has a stake, a choice—that they have to intervene otherwise things are going to get worse. He gives an example to elucidate his point: In jail Binayak used to listen to news about Gaza on his radio, and he compares the situation there with what is currently happening in Chhattisgarh—people being treated like objects. Thousands killed, so many useless deaths in a small place. "Any human being today who calls himself civilized, educated, should answer, How did Gaza happen and to what extent was I responsible? You cannot have human life valued greatly in this pocket and not in that pocket," his voice has risen in anger, then he softens to add, "Human beings need to believe that our sufferings have some significance."

And as is common knowledge by now, despite personal threats much before his arrest, despite being beaten up, his jeep being surrounded, his family witnessing this physical intimidation many times, Binayak was among the first to make that choice, raise his voice, go to an area of displacement and violence—Bastar—and record injustice and then make it public.

People have to raise their voices *collectively* for peace and say we will not countenance war, we will not countenance military confrontation as a way for imposing solutions—that is not legitimate, whether the state is doing it or others. This movement has to gain impetus on its own and become a much larger thing, says Binayak.

"But you have a voice now, and whether you accept it or not, greatness has been thrust upon you, why *don't* you want to take on the mantle?" I ask gently.

He shrugs his shoulders and smiles deprecatingly, "I didn't formulate any mathematical equations, I didn't bring about any new ideas in physics, I didn't write a book (laughs and shakes his head, teasing me a little)...these are things I consider...I haven't written any music, these are things that are worthy of greatness. Of course I think ordinary people *also* do great things. They bring up children to face the world, they make love...I think those things are great. I think listening to good singing, music, sitting around, chatting with one's children is also great," he defies me to disagree.

But *he's* the crusading defender of people's rights and freedom, isn't he?

If everyone does it, then there's any point of my doing it, Binayak says, somewhat wearily.

He doesn't want to be a prophet in the wilderness anymore, he says firmly. He wants to do what he has always done best, be a part of a large group of friends who believe that this is not the right way to go forward, not the way for India to become a better place to live in. And *then* work together towards change.

Some of Binayak's ideas are already in the pipeline. Since late 2009 he has started giving lecture tours all over the country— Patna, Aligarh, Chennai, Kolkata, Mumbai—to activists, students, social organizations, academic institutions on issues closest to his heart and work—health and human rights. The larger goal, to build a mass movement for peace and justice, as he has been reiterating since his release from jail in May 2009, is accompanied by the equally strong desire to create awareness among the uninitiated about issues like dispossession and hunger, problems that are not unique to Chhattisgarh but faced by millions of Indians for decades.

Yet this is not his primary field of work, and during our September meeting when I went to observe his trial proceedings, his matter-of-fact statement that it's hard for people who are always engaged in work to be disengaged for such long periods, hits me with the force of a sledgehammer, more due to its even tone of delivery and complete lack of self-pity.

Three months later I watch him mingle with the faculty and students of Xaviers college, Mumbai, where he is a keynote speaker at a human rights seminar. The next day he will deliver a lecture at the Tata Institute for Social Sciences. Between the lectures is an informal meeting with the Mumbai group of the Free Binayak Sen campaign, the first after his release.

Unobtrusively observing him interact with the many people who come forward to meet him, some friends but mostly strangers, I get the feeling that for Binayak, this is a role that does not really come naturally. He is pursuing it diligently, as is his wont, because it is part of the civil society peace agenda he wants to systematically build, create awareness about issues that he wants others to participate in, but going out there, being in the spotlight, listening to the applause, sitting through flattering introductions, is something he quickly steps over, moving immediately ahead with his prepared speech.

This is a completely new avatar of Binayak Sen, or at least one that I have never seen or heard about in all of my conversations with the people who know him well. Reading out his speech from notes in front of him, Binayak is nevertheless, a forceful, passionate, engrossing speaker, keeping the mostly youthful, totally urban audience engaged, that too in near-total silence for the duration of his talk. The lecture itself is an interestingly woven mix of the essence of what he himself stands for, health and human rights. He begins by reading out a text message sent to him by VCA activist Himanshu Kumar (who had earlier also lectured at the same venue) about his associate Kopa Kunjam and lawyer Alwin Toppo being picked up for questioning by the Bijapur police. He also tells the audience about advocate and activist Sudha Bhardwaj and a team of women activists being beaten up on their way to Narayanpatna in Orissa to investigate human rights abuses there, explaining that events that are being discussed are simultaneously happening. The ominous news brings home the immediacy and urgency of what he goes on to say, like nothing else can, he and his friends are living out what everyone else discusses as a "situation that is getting out of control." And a vast majority don't even know what is going on in a part of India that they don't really care about.

Binayak is here in Mumbai, in an elite college, to try and change that.

He talks of having the unique privilege of "reading the politics of his patients off their bodies", of how the thin, starved bodies tell their own stories of neglect and despair, of deprivation and poverty. He talks of his own area of specialization, paediatrics and nutrition, of how 45 per cent of Indian children are malnourished, that adults are malnourished too. He quotes data from the National Monitoring Bureau in Hyderabad: 33 per cent of the adult population in the country have a body mass index (BMI) of less than 18.5, more than 50 per cent of scheduled tribes and more than 60 per cent of scheduled castes have a BMI below 18.5. This, according to the WHO criterion, is a community in famine. This 33 per cent were malnourished yesterday, are malnourished today and will be malnourished tomorrow. The first word therefore is famine, says Binayak to the silent audience. The second word is war, and he then describes the Salwa Judum, as per the investigation conducted by the coalition of human rights organization in November 2005, and the report they published in April 2006, titled "When the State Wages War Against Its Own People". He reads out an excerpt that describes the plight of the homeless tribals:

"Tens and thousands of people are now refugees in temporary roadside camps or living with relatives with complete disruption of their daily lives. Prospects for their return are currently dim. The entire operation instead of being a peace machine as it is claimed, has escalated violence on all sides. However only the murders by Maoists have been recognized and the Salwa Judum and the paramilitary operate with complete impunity. The rule of law has completely broken down. People who are already in a state of famine, they survive as a result of a tenuous and fragile equilibrium which they have achieved with their own ecological reality. And by subjecting them to displacement with the backing of arms, these people are rendered not only homeless but they are separated from the fragile support base on which their lives are conducted from day-to-day."

The logical outcome of the first two processes brings him to the third word, says Binayak firmly: genocide, which does not only mean killing people. He reads from the United Nations Convention on the Prevention and Punishment of the Crime of Genocide which defines genocide as deliberately inflicting on the group conditions of life calculated to bring about its physical destruction in part or whole. He argues that what is happening in Bastar, Chhattisgarh falls well within the crime of genocide and it's not a simple matter of the adivasis being ground between the Maoists and the state forces, as the media and others keep emphasizing. The political reality of the identity of the adivasis, their long history, their rich culture, the way they lived happily without poverty earlier, all of this has to be recognized.

He ends by reading from "Violence Today", quoting statistics again, saying that in the last six years, more children have died globally as a result of starvation and preventable diseases than humans perished in the six years of the Second World War. All Binayak wants to stress when he quotes statistics to lend weightage to his statements and arguments is the contrast—every three seconds that a human life ceases to exist, in the same three seconds, 1,20,000 dollars are spent worldwide on military armaments. What is more important, he is silently asking you to question, when you go back home after listening to his lecture, a peaceful harmonious existence or more and more stock-piling of military arms in preparation for armed conflict and increased violence? He says that resistance only becomes a necessity in the face of outrageous injustice, of the self-enrichment of the mega rich and the increasing impoverishment of broad segments of society. In closing he quotes Bertolt Brecht, "You have to resist if you don't want to perish".

Watching him wait to field questions from the audience, I wonder how much of an effect his words have had on the constituency he is trying to break into, the urban middle class, the youth, the educated people of the country who can join him in his mission. I scan the faces of the people around me. It is hard to gauge interest from reactions to a lecture, howsoever inspiring or insightful. It is after all, a world far removed from the one they inhabit, the reality they know or encounter daily.

And then the first question comes, predictably curious, asked by a young student, "What was your life like when you were in prison?" Binayak patiently answers, giving details about the inequalities of life inside prison, the lack of legal aid for the poor, the several cases of total injustice he learnt about, the friends he made, the horrifying beatings by *lambardars* of prisoners, the terrible food. Everyone listens to the stories, awestruck.

A few more questions follow, mostly inane ones and then it's time for Binayak to leave and for me to follow him to the Mumbai Union of Journalists' office where his Mumbai core supporters' team is waiting to cheer his release, much like the PUCL meeting in Raipur in September. This is basically bonding time, informal discussions with friends like lawyers Sanobar Keshwaar and Kamayani Mahabal Bali, documentary film maker Anand Patwardhan, journalist Jyoti Punwani and various activists.

~

Creating awareness about Chhattisgarh's human rights issues, displacement, the Maoist battle, the increased clashes with security forces, seems quite a challenge to me and I recall Himanshu Kumar's lecture delivered at another elite Mumbai college, Sophia Polytechnic, Social Communications Media department, in November 2009.

He too spoke passionately, his words laced with emotion and warning, "All of us are responsible for the silent support we give to the government to treat the tribals the way they do. This is the sequestration of natural resources, I am better off so I should get more, these are the socially accepted norms. I live in Mumbai so I should get more than a person living in Bastar. This is violence but we don't see it because we are beneficiaries of this value system. Those who are outside it, who are being targeted, being raped and killed, they will destroy it. You want peace, they want justice, the priorities are different."

Like Binayak, Himanshu has been a grassroots worker, helping tribals in Bastar with their day-to-day issues of livelihood for seventeen years till the Salwa Judum disrupted his life and more literally his Vanvasi Chetna Ashram as well. So when he articulates the ground reality in Bastar, it is a heartfelt plea for understanding, for people to care, and this is why he and Binayak are travelling to cities across India, lecturing at college campuses and civil society meetings, creating a mass base for a mass movement for peace and justice.

Himanshu's brutally frank words and passionate delivery stun the media students of Sophia's Polytechnic into near total silence. He completes his lecture with a severe indictment of a corporate-funded media which does not report atrocities on tribals, a parliament where not a single MP is willing to take up the issue because corporates fund 25 per cent of each election and an apathetic public which prefers to watch *saas-bahu* television soaps and 20-20 cricket matches, secure in the illusion that all is well. Who needs adivasis, who cares if they live or die?

But there were people who *did* care, who had worked in the area with those same adivasis, watched them face large-scale displacement from their homes and fields, first at the hands of the Salwa Judum from 2005 onwards and then, from October 2009 onwards at the hands of increased militarization or what would be later termed, Operation Green Hunt. They planned a systematic campaign to protect the tribals and simultaneously protest against what was happening in Bastar. Dantewada was the chosen area since it was the most affected and Himanshu was the natural choice to be one of the more visible faces of the campaign and lead a *padayatra* from December 14-25, 2009 that was to pass through seventeen villages. The objective was to restore much-needed confidence among the tribals who only saw more and more military power troop into their lives every day. How did it matter to them whether it was state power or central power, whether any minister (notably Home Minister P. Chidambaram) denied it as Operation Green Hunt or not, whether it was in the name of battling Maoists or "area domination"? Their lives had changed irrevocably due to the intrusive security presence and the human rights abuses. This, in addition to what they endured on a daily basis in any case—hunger, lack of basic amenities like health care, education etc. The *padayatra* was meant to document all of these issues.

It never happened.

Himanshu was forbidden to step into a single village without police armed escort. He was labelled a threat to the very villages he had once worked in.

A rally was planned in Dantewada on December 25, 2009 to bring together people from all over the country to raise a voice against displacement of tribals and the on-going war-like situation in the region.

This too never happened.

The *Jan Sunwai* or people's court of tribals' grievances, was to be held on January 7, 2010. It was to be witnessed by a panel of former justices, bureaucrats, journalists and activists, and was agreed upon by Chidambaram in a meeting with Himanshu Kumar in November 2009 so that he could hear first-hand the truth about the atrocities committed by the Salwa Judum.

This also did not happen.

The thirty odd activists from NAPM and other organizations, including Medha Patkar and Sandeep Pandey who came to Dantewada to attend the *Jan Sunwai,* were heckled, pelted with eggs, attacked by a large gang of Salwa Judum supporters who accused the activists of being Naxal sympathizers. The lone local television channel recording this fracas telecast only fragments of Medha's protesting speech saying she spoke on behalf of the tribals. The larger issue of atrocities or the on-going repression in the area remained an untold story.

Stray intrepid reporters from Mumbai who went to Dantewada to cover the *Jan Sunwai* were assaulted, their cameras confiscated. All this so that nobody would find out what was happening to people exploited and abused for a long time without being noticed.

Binayak spoke out strongly against the aborted *padayatra*, the rally and assault on Medha Patkar and Sandeep Pandey and the no-show at the *Jan Sunwai* but his voice too remain largely unheard, his protest recorded on "theothermedia.org" website, an alternate media website not known to all.

Dantewada was still off the map of India.

The fact that it was the first area to be the target of Operation Green Hunt—an internal military offensive launched by the Central Government in the forests of Chhattisgarh, Jharkhand, Orissa, Andhra Pradesh and West Bengal—was not widely known. Neither was the marching in of an additional seven battalions of Central forces in Bastar, bringing the total number of troops to 20,000, to "secure the roads, enter the villages, sanitise operations," to "clear and hold". These were terms used by government officials who described the operation as taking back control of land which had been captured by Maoists and restoring civil administration such as the PDS (public distribution scheme), schools and clinics. None of these had been functioning for a long while (as stated in the PUCL report "When the State Wages War Against Its Own People") in any case, in Bastar in the first place.

In this plan of "recovering areas", as many as twenty jungle warfare training schools were planned to be set up (three are already functioning, including one in Kanker, 200 kilometres from Raipur), a large amount of military supplies and global positioning systems technology were purchased, more and more troops— COBRA (Commando Battalion for Resolute Action), state police and paramilitary forces—were sent into the adivasi villages of Bastar. The stage was set for what people like Himanshu Kumar and Binayak Sen had been publicly warning everyone about for over six months, the danger of structural violence—expending effort and energy to keep inequity in place. It had all the makings of a civil war.

Operation Green Hunt would inevitably lead to more of what its precursor, the Salwa Judum, had ensured for Bastar's adivasis.

The corporates, both Indian and international, were still waiting. Mittal, Vedanta, Tata, Essar, Jindal, Posco, waiting to mine the tribals' lands for riches like bauxite, coal, iron ore that lay beneath.

This, according to the commonly held belief, was after all, the primary goal behind the evacuation of the 644 villages over the five years since the inception of the Salwa Judum. The fact that the 5th Schedule of the Indian Constitution grants the tribals complete rights over their traditional land and forests, prohibiting companies from mining it, would not apply if there were no villagers occupying that land.

And so, marginalized, poor, displaced people already having faced indiscriminate arrests, torture, harassment, rape, fake encounters at the hands of the state and summary execution at the hands of the Maoists for the crime of "being informers or suspected informers", were now in for Round Two.

By January 2010, Himanshu Kumar was driven out of Dantewada, asked to vacate the rented house he lived in, warned that nobody in Dantewada would be allowed to rent him a place to stay in and after seventeen years, his organization, the VCA disbanded. The VCA volunteers continue their rehabilitation work but under other names they help other organizations. Himanshu hopes to re-start the centre one day. In the interim, he has relocated to a destination unknown and continues his campaign for awareness, undeterred.

The conflict between the state and the Maoists in Chhattisgarh also continues, both sides claiming their own victories and territories. The Maoists claim to run a parallel government where only their writ runs, complete with arms and ammunition and popular support. The state sends in more troops in joint operations to "reclaim" those areas of Maoist control. G K Pillai, India's Home Secretary declared that 5,000 sq km had been "recovered" in Rajnandgaon and Kanker (in Chhattisgarh) and that civil administration had been restored.

On February 22, 2010, Kishenji, CPI (Maoist) leader, issued a ceasefire call for seventy-two days. The very next day, a forum called the Citizens for Peace and Justice, led by Justice Rajindar Sachar, writer Arundhati Roy, senior advocate Prashant Bhushan and others, issued a statement to the Central Government asking for its intervention in talks with the CPI (Maoist) and welcoming the ceasefire offer by the Maoists.

Their other demands included a halt to Operation Green Hunt, cessation of hostilities on both sides, the honouring of the 5th Schedule of the Constitution, freezing of all MOUs signed, and allowing observers and human rights groups to go to the affected areas.

~

Seven months may have seen tumultuous change in Chhattisgarh, the unfolding of the dangerous situation that Binayak foretold but his stance has not changed at all. Resistance to displacement (of the tribals in Bastar) is the only way to survive, he says, otherwise the government's continued policy of displacement will only lead to a kinder, gentler genocide where people will die of hunger (and every indignity possible) rather than bullets.

I think about the thin line Binayak treads between idealism and inevitability. The answers he provides are generic, they do not specify any particular plan of action. But I keep my thoughts to myself, we have had these discussions before, he still believes in his people-driven agenda for peace with justice and I still respect that belief, it is rare enough to find it today.

He tells me about his current project with CMC, Vellore academics. They are working on the interface of health and human rights in the training of a new generation of doctors. This will then be included in their syllabus.

When I want to know whether he misses being the doctor he was once famous for being, his practice, his patients still patiently waiting for him at Bagrumnala, he says health care is much more than examining patients and prescribing medicines. He quotes Rudolph Virchow: "Politics is medicine writ large." Today health and human rights have to take on dimensions larger than individual bio-medical interventions, he adds. It is a measure of how much I am beginning to know him that I anticipate an answer very much similar to the one I get!

At the same time, he still hopes to start where he left off in Bagrumnala some day soon.

The seven month period interspersed with five meetings and several telephone conversations has forged a bond of sorts between the two of us, Binayak and I. One that is hard to define, harder to share really. It is even more difficult to answer my own question of how much of the Binayak Sen story I have been able to uncover—what started off as a journey of discovery didn't quite end the way I had pictured it in my mind. All the pieces neatly fitting in, a story with a clear-cut beginning, middle and end, the way it is supposed to be. Binayak Sen doesn't quite fit the mould.

What comes to light through conversations both with him and about him is the essence of his personality, his belief and value system, choices taken, his commitment to the road he decided to travel on, and beneath the gentle exterior and calm tones, an unshakeable will. This is a man who will achieve what he sets out to do, regardless of obstacles or consequences; if he is doing what he believes is the right thing to do.

I think of the apocryphal story told to me about how he grew a beard after the demolition of the Babri Masjid to experience what it meant to be part of a minority. Binayak confirms this, saying he had read a book called "Black Like Me" about a white man who puts on black make-up and travels all over America to try and see what it feels like to be a black man. Binayak found this very instructive, wanted to have the same experience and he did! This is the extent to which he can go to empathize with someone else's pain.

But today he seems strangely reluctant to take on a larger role than the one he has adopted—lecturing, touring the country, speaking of health and human rights, malnutrition and famine, the need for peace with justice and equity—an invisible line seems to have been drawn somewhere. Or maybe people just expect more from him than he wants or is able to deliver. They compare him to Gandhi, refer to him as a modern Gandhi, but I refrain from mentioning this to Binayak. He would only have got annoyed and dismissed it.

The rest of it is easy—Binayak the foodie, Binayak the singer, the lover of Rabindra Sangeet, reciting poetry aloud, a caring father, a supportive husband, a solicitous host.

These are the surface level, visible, charming aspects of his essentially "loner" persona (one of his CMC professors also corroborates my impression). A disarming smile can catch you unawares, a hearty laugh is rare but most likely when elder daughter Pranhita mimics a colleague. When the entire family is together, with Binayak cooking a simple egg *bhurji* to add to the meal, there is shared laughter, most of it courtesy Pranhita's gregariousness, Ilina's anecdotes, Binayak's wit.

But there are other occasions I remember too, when he and I have travelled in almost total silence in a car simply because he had nothing he wanted to say to me in particular! He is affectionate though, demonstrably so, greeting me with a warm hug after a rapport had been established after perhaps the second meeting or so. A little later, during two successive unscheduled surgeries that I needed to undergo, he regularly asked about my recovery, the medication I was on, why I wasn't feeling better, reassuring me with words of encouragement. You can easily agree with the vast number of people who praise his compassion. He is an extremely good listener too, drawing people out with confidences they have no idea they are revealing.

Essentially however it was a working relationship and began and ended as one, though I would have liked to be counted as one of Binayak's friends, I know that I am not, I do not even call him Binayak. (Ilina on the other hand, is someone with whom I establish a first-name basis within weeks of meeting, she is far more friendly!) He teases me about it during that last meeting, "You are the only person in the world who calls me Dr Sen."

I reply that when I started working on the book, I was addressing him as "Sir" and thought perhaps I would end up calling him Binayak, but clearly that did not happen. Dr Sen is what I will continue to call him.

He is most comfortable when I talk to him about work, not so much when, in summation, I mention his body of work, preferring to attribute it once again to "collective" team efforts.

To the also-inevitable question of whether he ever thought of taking the easier path, he is disarmingly frank and laughs, "Many times", he says. The option of taking an easier path is always open and when the costs are paid by loved ones like family, friends and associates, one always thinks of alternative scenarios where those difficulties could have been avoided, that is only human, and Binayak is not ashamed to admit to being human.

But of course in the end or in the beginning, for that matter, Binayak did not take the easier option, not then and not now.

He says simply that in the fight of truth versus falsehood everyone has to choose and he chose the only path he could.

I leave the Wardha house, promising to meet him next for the film shoot in the first week of April. He wishes me good luck and I walk out feeling strangely bereft, a little like I felt after the first meeting back in July 2009, but this time the journey is over, the story is complete.

But in the state of Chhattisgarh the story is far from over.

~

When I call him to finalize shooting dates on April 2, he tells me that the Bagrumnala clinic will be formally re-started on April 18 and we could plan accordingly.

~

Four days later, in the early hours of April 6, seventy-six policemen of the CRPF's A company and a state head constable were ambushed and killed in Dantewada by Maoists, clearly and literally perched at an advantage. The column of eighty-one CRPF men were on the second day of the "area domination" patrol in the Mukrana forest, hadn't been trained in jungle warfare and were victims of what would be termed India's worst counter-insurgency disaster.

Dantewada was suddenly front-page, national news, meriting twenty-four-hour coverage.

From initially mispronouncing the name itself to finally sending reporters to what television news channels insisted on calling Ground Zero, Dantewada was the story everybody was suddenly eager to tell. It was being termed the epicentre of a war.

Detailed analysis of the three hour-plus encounter with the hopelessly trapped and beleagured CRPF jawans, survivor accounts of the remaining jawans who mentioned sari-clad tribal women and even children collecting ammunition off the bodies of the dead, heart-rending tales of grieving families and disturbingly haunting images of seventy six coffins wrapped in the Indian tri-color—these were just some of the recurring motifs in the media in the days that followed the Dantewada massacre.

Tapping into the pervasive public anger, a few hours after the bloodbath, Chidambaram said the state would launch an all-out offensive against the Maoists since they had declared war. "We might lose more people, many more may die, it might take two-three years but ultimately the state will prevail," he declared firmly.

Equally combative statements were issued by the DIG, anti-Naxal operations, Dantewada, S R P Kalluri, "We had cleared that area, now we will have to sanitize it again."

Wipe them out, send in the army, what is all this talk about root causes, about development...these were the standard, high-pitched responses in political and media debates, human rights activists were scornfully asked to respond, to denounce the Maoist violence.

Arundhati Roy retaliated by travelling to the Dandakaranya forests with the Maoists and writing a thirty-three page article in Outlook magazine, calling the Maoists "Gandhians with Guns".

Mainstream media went all out with its coverage of the massacre and its implications. Maps were shown depicting the Red Corridor exceeding 45,000 sq km over five states in the country, 234 districts in India, areas of Maoist domination, manned by approximately 60,000 policemen, fighting an estimated 15,000 Maoist militants, fighting a losing battle nonetheless.

Discussions on how the state crushed the Naxal movement thrice in the past—in West Bengal, in Bihar and in Andhra Pradesh, at great human cost—of how the Maoists resurrected themselves, of whether it truly was the "greatest internal security threat" as declared by Prime Minister Manmohan Singh, what were the solutions, what was the way out, continued all week long on television and in newspapers and magazines.

Till some other Breaking News took precedence and civil war or the threat of it in Chhattisgarh receeded to the back burner once again.

Five days after the Dantewada killings, Binayak Sen issued a statement, published in "The Hindu", condemning the processes of violence and militarisation that led to the deaths of seventy six police personnel, but he also spoke about the deaths of many people on both sides of the ongoing conflict between the Maoists and the state forces, the attendant tragic deaths of so many ordinary citizens that went unrecorded and largely un-mourned.

Once again he appealed for the cessation of violence and the beginning of political dialogue for the peace with equity and justice that he has been seeking and speaking about tirelessly.

He was also perhaps the only human rights activist in India to condemn the Dantewada massacre.

Unfortunately for Binayak and for his patients, the tumultuous turn of events prevented him from re-starting his Bagrumnala clinic. Plans had to be changed once more, the "too much change" that Ilina had spoken of six months back in Vellore had become a constant reality.

On a national level the aftermath of the Dantewada attack continued to have a ripple effect. The buck stops at my desk, declared P. Chidambaram, offering to resign over Dantewada in Parliament where heated debates took place over two days, over accountability and blame, with both Opposition leaders and Congressmen scoring political points over a tragic event. In the end, the Home Minister stayed on, to later issue a warning to all those who spoke in favour of Maoist guerillas—they would face legal action and ten years in jail, under the Unlawful Activities (Prevention) Act (UAPA).

This diktat from the Home ministry warned "certain NGOs and intellectuals who support the CPI-Maoist ideology" that the CPI-Maoist and all its front organizations had been designated as terrorist groups.

~

E N Rammohan, former Director-General of the BSF submitted his report of the inquiry he conducted at the Home Ministry's behest, into the Dantewada massacre. He told the press that the Maoists cannot be overcome by sheer force alone, that there were several flaws in the ongoing anti-insurgency operations, that the entire approach was wrong, joint operations between the paramilitary forces and state police were a mistake, tribals should first be given their due and that it was a socio-economic issue for which a military solution was unacceptable.

The report was not publicized and its contents not made public. The action recommended, punishment for not following the correct procedure by the CRPF, was not followed up.

Nothing changed in the state of Chhattisgarh.

A month after the Dantewada episode, eight CRPF personnel were killed by Naxals in the same state. In an official statement, the CPI-Maoist warned of more attacks like Dantewada unless the "fascist mindset refused to see the socio-politico-economic root causes of Naxalism".

Nobody spoke about a political dialogue anymore.

In the meantime, Binayak had been elected President of the Chhattisgarh PUCL, with Sudha Bharadwaj taking on the post he formerly occupied, of General Secretary. But with the suspension of civil liberties and by extension, any meaningful activism under the Unlawful Activities Prevention Act, this new responsibility comes with a truly difficult dimension attached.

In view of the changed scenario, I send Binayak a fresh set of questions. I ask him about the future of human rights activism in the country and in Chhattisgarh in particular, given the new restrictions. As the newly elected President of Chhattisgarh's PUCL will he not face trouble with the state once again?

His answer is characteristically simple, even though at the moment the future for strong activism seems bleak as it always has been when fascism gains ground, despite all the difficulties, he continues to believe that reason and humanity will prevail. That the call for peace will gain force and cogency only when it is taken up by large sections of society as a whole.

Others may describe him as an icon for peace, a calm and compassionate person who would make a fine leader but Binayak sees himself only as a participant in the struggle he wants everyone to join in.

Binayak Sen was looking forward to leading a normal life when I first met him, two months after his release from a two-year incarceration in jail.

Today he is no closer to finding that normal life, but continues to search for it in the everyday reality of life. His strength, as always, comes from the sustaining belief that in times of travail, thousands are suffering, one is not alone.

On May 14, 2010, I scan the newspapers and watch the television news channels all day for even a mention, a marking of the third anniversary of Binayak Sen's arrest, since the trial is still going on and he continues to be one of India's most famous political prisoners.

Apart from an interview conducted by a little-known radio/TV channel called Democracy Now, based in the US, faithfully posted on the Free Binayak Sen site on Facebook by Kamayani Mahabal, nobody has remembered Binayak Sen.

The story, the campaign, the movement is over.

It is now up to the man alone to take forward all the goodwill, the hope, the expectations, the faith that a lot of us, including me, continue to repose in him.

That final choice is once again Binayak Sen's call.